Hydraulic vs Electric

THE BATTLE FOR THE BR DIESEL FLEET

David N. Clough

Ian Allan
PUBLISHING

Front cover (upper): Perhaps the most fondly remembered of all BR's diesel-hydraulic locomotives are the lightweight 'Warships', based on an existing German design. Here Swindon-built No D829 *Magpie* passes Basingstoke with a Waterloo–Exeter express on 27 June 1966. *Gavin Morrison*

Front cover (lower): One of the most successful diesel-electric designs built for BR was the English Electric Type 3, better known today as Class 37. No D6736 is seen at Doncaster Works when brand-new on 29 April 1962. *Gavin Morrison*

Back cover (upper): The first of Freightliner's Class 70s, the latest diesel-electric locomotives to enter service in the UK, built in the USA by General Electric. *Freightliner*

Back cover (lower): The prototype Voith Maxima 4000, representing the current state of the art in the design of main-line diesel-hydraulic locomotives. *Voith*

Below: Built in 1955 as a private venture by English Electric, *Deltic* was at the time of its construction the world's most powerful diesel locomotive. Seen here heading an up express near Peascliffe, north of Grantham, during August 1960, it impressed the Eastern Region's management, which persuaded BR to order a fleet of 22 production locomotives for use on the East Coast main line. *J. S. Hancock*

First published 2011

ISBN 978 0 7110 3550 8

Published by Ian Allan Publishing

an imprint of Ian Allan Publishing Ltd, Hersham, Surrey, KT12 4RG

Printed in England by Ian Allan Printing Ltd, Hersham, Surrey, KT12 4RG

Code: 1102/B2

Distributed in the United States of America and Canada by BookMasters Distribution Services

Visit the Ian Allan Publishing website at www.ianallanpublishing.com

CONTENTS

FOREWORD

When I met Peter Waller, Ian Allan Publishing's commissioning editor, in my 19th-floor office overlooking Manchester's city centre during July 2008, we discussed the substantial quantity of historical material I was unearthing in the National Archives at Kew. Some of it was finding its way into the *BR Standard Diesels* project then drawing to a close, but we felt there was potential to bring more of the information into the public arena, because the documents revealed quite a different perspective on the events surrounding the 'dieselisation' of British Railways. The upshot of this debate is the present title.

I am perhaps best known for my long association with Class 50, and some partisan diesel-hydraulic enthusiasts hold a mistaken belief that I am opposed to that form of traction. In truth this is far from the case; in my view the Class 35 'Hymeks' are probably the most underrated diesel type ever owned by British Railways and were only overshadowed because of the success of Class 37, arguably British Railways' second-most-successful design. I have also often wondered why the flagship class — the 'D1000' 'Westerns' — showed up so badly when compared to the rival Brush Type 4, while there was the broader issue of why diesel-hydraulic designs that worked well in Germany were not so good when replicated in Britain.

When Peter suggested a book examining the relative merits of diesel-electric and diesel-hydraulic transmission I was at first keen, but then the magnitude of the task dawned, not least because the innermost workings of hydraulic drive were something of a mystery to me! What emerged quickly was the lack of any description of this topic in many of the standard works on the subject, so here was a deficiency to address in the book.

Main-line traction has not been confined to electric or hydraulic drive, powered by a diesel engine. There have been notable experiments with gas-turbine propulsion, while the diesel-mechanical option has been employed in a line-service locomotive, as well as in numerous railcars and multiple-units; thus the debate needed to consider why certain types of transmission did or did not work in certain applications, and this, of necessity, must include the railcar, the diesel multiple-unit and the diesel trainset.

I am not an engineer and have no engineering training. This means that I have to be able to get to grips with some at times highly technical subject matter, and to try to impart the information in a way that fellow lay readers can comprehend, as well as offering sufficient depth for those with a thirst for the fine detail.

Of course, this is not just a story about the Western Region's diesel-hydraulic types in operation. As noted already, the genesis for this project was the information culled from the British Railways files at the National Archives, the vast majority of which had not previously been put into the public domain. Of prime importance has been the emergence of a time-line for diesel-hydraulic locomotives that is quite at variance with the perceived wisdom. Other background research, principally from the *Railway Gazette* dating back to 1933, has fleshed out points of historical relevance. Perhaps a subtitle for this book might be 'Overturning the Myths and Legends about the Western Region's diesel-hydraulics', because, for sure, much that has been written previously on this subject has not borne scrutiny against official records. I have been assiduous in referencing within the text, so that those who consider that I have got it all wrong can go and check for themselves. This is something other writers on the subject have never done, so identifying from where they have obtained their research on specific points is impossible.

Although this book is about the ebb and flow of the two forms of transmission in Great Britain, events here were influenced, to a greater or lesser degree, by developments overseas, particularly in Germany and the USA. It has, therefore, been essential to refer to what was happening in these countries at critical stages in diesel traction development in order to arrive at a balanced picture.

ACKNOWLEDGEMENTS

I have received the assistance of Clive Burrows, a railway engineer at the top of his profession and a man with very detailed knowledge of the Western Region diesel fleet from the 1970s. His input in key aspects has proved invaluable. Jeremy Clarke was one of the Western Region's diesel-locomotive engineers between 1963 and 1989, having responsibility for the region's fleet from 1981, and he too has been able to add much value. Richard Holmes is one of the current crop of engineers; his intimate knowledge of modern railcars and DMUs has enabled the story to be brought up to date. Wolfgang Paetzold worked for Voith Turbo until 1995, when he retired as Chief Engineering Manager of the rail division. During the relevant period he represented Voith in the 'D1000' project and has direct knowledge of events at the time. After his retirement Voith commissioned him to write a complete history of the company's rail traction activities. Herr Paetzold has been most kind in answering specific questions about the 'D1000' class, as well as translating key parts of his Voith history. The involvement of the four men mentioned here means there has been no need to rely on the writings of others about the Western Region diesel-hydraulics; rather, what follows is observations from those who knew the locomotives at first hand. Philip Heathcote has contributed to the German translations. Joe Burr rendered assistance in explaining the advantages of AC drive systems in diesel locomotives. Last, but by no means least, my wife, Jo, has provided considerable assistance in research and proofing.

David N. Clough
Leigh
November 2010

ABBREVIATIONS

bhp	brake horsepower
BR	British Railways, later British Rail
BRCW	Birmingham Railway Carriage & Wagon Co
BTC	British Transport Commission
CCE	Chief Civil Engineer
CM&EE	Chief Mechanical & Electrical Engineer
CME	Chief Mechanical Engineer
DB	Deutsche Bundesbahn (German Federal Railways) (*now Deutsche Bahn*)
DMU	diesel multiple-unit
ECML	East Coast main line
edhp	equivalent drawbar horsepower (*hp at locomotive drawbar, corrected for the gradient*)
EMU	electric multiple-unit
GM	General Motors
GWR	Great Western Railway
hp	horsepower
ILocoE	Institution of Locomotive Engineers
IMechE	Institution of Mechanical Engineers
KM	Krauss-Maffei
LMR	London Midland Region
LMS	London, Midland & Scottish Railway
LNER	London & North Eastern Railway
MAN	Maschinenfabrik Augsburg-Nürnberg
Metrovick	Metropolitan Vickers Electrical Co
mpc	miles per casualty
mph	miles per hour
NBL	North British Locomotive Co Ltd
Paxman	Davey Paxman & Co
rhp	rail horsepower
rpm	revolutions per minute
SR	Southern Railway, later Southern Region
WCML	West Coast main line
WR	Western Region

1

THE REPLACEMENT
OF STEAM

Early developments

The steam locomotive is not a particularly efficient prime mover. It converts less than 10% of the calorific value of its fuel into propulsion, and it has to be manned by a crew of two. Preparation and disposal at the start and end of duty are time-consuming and messy; there is no 'start' button for instant operation. Of course, steam locomotives are cheaper to manufacture than the alternatives, and need simpler, cheaper maintenance regimes. The fuel — usually coal — was also plentiful and cheap in Britain up to the 1950s, while that other essential component to steam traction's operating cycle — water — was not in short supply.

Railway administrations were generally alive to economies in operating practices. It was therefore natural for them to consider alternatives to steam traction, once these began to become available, especially as they permitted single-manning when labour was no longer cheap or readily available. The beginning of the end of steam on the over-ground railways in Britain can be traced to the projects of the pre-Grouping companies, which electrified some suburban routes during the early years of the 20th century.

In the same period a few petrol-engined rail vehicles also appeared in Britain. One of the first emerged as a result of the CME of the Great Central Railway's being impressed by a lightweight vehicle that he had seen while on a visit to Hungary. By this date such railcars were being developed to a much greater extent on the Continent than in Britain. The British Westinghouse Electric Manufacturing Co Ltd was commissioned to build a petrol-electric, self-propelled, double-bogied railcar. A 90hp petrol engine drove a dynamo, which supplied current to two Westinghouse traction motors mounted on one bogie. Some equipment, including the radiators, was roof-mounted. After trials the vehicle entered traffic on 28 March 1912 in the London area of the Great Central. Although 50mph was attainable, the maximum speed on level track was 40mph. Capable of towing a coach, this pioneer survived into the 1930s.

The first diesel-powered main-line locomotive was tried out on the Prussian State Railway in Germany in 1913. A design collaboration between Sulzer, Klose and Dr Rudolf Diesel himself, this 1,000hp locomotive had a direct-drive transmission between the engine and the wheels, an arrangement that proved unsuccessful.

Stirred by interest in this pioneer, General Electric of the USA set about designing a diesel-electric transmission and associated control gear. The result was the building after World War 1 of the USA's first diesel

The Westinghouse petrol-electric railcar, built to the order of the Great Central Railway. *Ian Allan Library*

locomotives, the GE-Ingersoll-Rand-Alco 300hp and 600hp units. During the 1920s progress was made with diesels of both slow- and quick-running types in Britain (Beardmore), elsewhere in Western Europe and in North America.

Progress in the 1930s — shunters

The first diesel locomotive ever to run on the railways of Britain was a 20-ton 0-4-0, with a Lentz hydrostatic transmission. It was built by the Grazer Waggon-und-Maschinenfabrik of Austria and spent two or three months on LNER metals during 1924 before returning to the maker.

It took until around 1930 for diesel engine and electric drive technology to advance sufficiently to make this form of power generation a better option than the petrol engine for either main-line or shunting duties. To a greater or lesser degree, all the 'Big Four' post-Grouping railways flirted with diesel power, either for main-line applications or for shunting, using equipment from several engineering companies. Although this book focuses on main-line locomotives, it is worth remembering that much of the early application of diesel power in Britain was in the form of shunting locomotives.

For the first 10 years after World War 1, railways were fairly prosperous, but early in 1931 the President of the LMS, Sir Josiah Stamp, suggested that economies could be made, and that the possibility existed of exploring new and improved methods of operation. In October 1931 authority was given for the conversion of an 0-6-0 steam tank engine into an experimental shunting locomotive with a 400hp Paxman engine and a hydraulic transmission supplied by Haslam & Newton of Derby. Numbered 1831, it emerged from Derby Works in November 1932.

Before this locomotive was completed, Hunslet had built a diesel shunter, and facilities were given by the LMS for it to be tried in a goods yard adjoining the company's works. It went well: a shunting locomotive could be employed with advantage. Consequently authority was given for the purchase of about 12 examples of various types. Among these early prototypes the

Above: Pioneer LMS diesel shunter No 1831 stands at Derby on 20 July 1935, alongside an ex-Midland Railway Class 2P 4-4-0. *H. C. Casserley*

LMS's No 7078 of 1935 was built by the English Electric Co Ltd and featured the six-cylinder 'RK' series engine at 300-350hp; it was eventually selected to become the standard British Railways shunter, Class 08. Because they were distributed all over the system, the difficulties of training maintenance staff and drivers was very great, and an undue number of failures occurred, largely owing to drivers' unfamiliarity with the new type.

Despite the difficulties, the experiment was highly successful, and out of it two important results emerged. First, from No 1831, the importance of providing a double-reduction gear was learned. Secondly, the use of the widely distributed smaller units fostered acceptance of the principle of one-man operation, without which no further development with one-man-operated shunting locomotives would have been possible.

Below: The LMS was not the only company in Britain to try diesel traction for shunting work. In 1944 the LNER built this prototype, No 8000, at Doncaster Works. *BR*

Railcars in Britain and Germany

In a paper delivered to the Institution of Locomotive Engineers on 23 January 1957 T. F. B. Simpson (Derby Works Manager) described his intimate involvement in 1928 with an experimental diesel-powered train that operated on the old Lancashire & Yorkshire section of the LMS in the Blackpool area. The author viewed this as the forerunner of what became in the 1950s the diesel multiple-unit. A 500hp high-speed Beardmore engine with an English Electric generator and equipment were installed in an experimental four-coach train, and it ran fairly successfully for a period, during which time valuable experience and knowledge was gained that was ultimately used in the development of the high-speed diesel engine, which was being commercially manufactured at the date of the paper. The Beardmore engine had been designed for airship applications, which rather mirrored events in Germany, notably with the Maybach Motorenbau company.

Back on the main line, Leyland Motors Ltd collaborated with the LMS during 1934 in the production of three railcars. They were specified by W. A. Stanier, the LMS CM&EE, and Leyland Motors Ltd carried out the detailed design and construction. A 130hp Leyland diesel was matched to a Leyland-Lysholm-Smith hydraulic transmission. A twin-axle wheelbase contributed to an overall weight of 10 tons for a seating capacity of 40; top speed was 56mph. Trials over the West Coast line as far as Carlisle proved successful, including climbing Shap, while a demonstration trip between Euston and Watford was made on 21 February 1934.

A Leyland railcar with a similar drive had already been at work on the Northern Counties Committee lines in Northern Ireland, which was part of the LMS. During a periodic examination in February 1934, the hydraulic drive had shown itself to be trouble-free and to need remarkably little maintenance.

Four years later, the *Railway Gazette* of 15 April 1938 described a three-car diesel-hydraulic train, with multiple-unit control, that had been built by the LMS at Derby. Leyland had developed a new diesel engine for railcar application, and it was used for the first time in this train. It had six cylinders, was of 8.6 litres capacity, and developed 125hp at 1,500rpm. Six engines were fitted to provide 750hp for the trainset. Each engine was coupled to a Leyland Lysholm hydraulic transmission. All these powertrains were mounted under the floor of the unit (two per vehicle), and each drove one axle. The driver had a throttle to control engine speed and a selector for choosing 'engine-only', hydraulic drive, or direct drive. The latter was for running at higher speeds, and 75mph was possible at maximum engine revolutions. Provision was made for seating 164 passengers, at an all-up weight that was less than half that of a steam-locomotive-hauled trainset of similar capacity. After some trial running, the unit was put into service on

In 1938 Derby built this three-car articulated diesel-hydraulic multiple-unit, the success of which inspired the use of the same type of powertrain in the first BR DMUs. *Ian Allan Library*

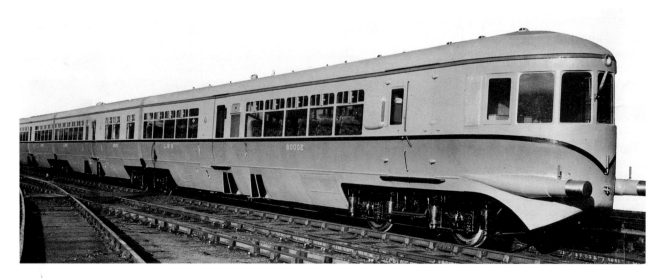

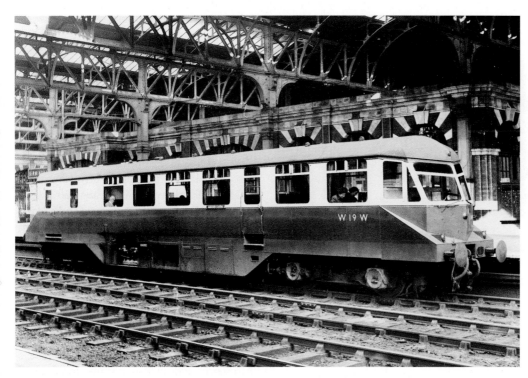

The GWR appreciated the advantages of diesel railcars in offering operating economy over steam. It used several types on country branch lines, on suburban duties and the cross-country route between Birmingham Snow Hill and Cardiff. Here car No 19 waits to leave Snow Hill on 28 October 1954 with the 2.27pm to Cheltenham. *Ian Allan Library*

12 September 1938 on the Oxford–Cambridge cross-country route.

In 1951 the Western Region produced a cross-departmental report on the performance of the ex-GWR railcars. Interestingly, the report states that they were introduced for the promotion of services for which there was only a limited demand; in other words, they were not seen as experimental. Railcar No 1 was built by AEC Ltd and had a single AEC 130hp bus engine. Service use began on 4 December 1933, with a single car based at Southall and providing additional services between there and Slough, Reading, Didcot and Oxford.

The success of the prototype led to an order in February 1934 for five additional, larger, higher-powered railcars; these were for fast supplementary business services on important cross-country routes. On 9 July 1934 railcars equipped with a buffet appeared on the Birmingham Snow Hill–Cardiff route, for which an extra 2s 6d (12½p) was charged above the standard fare. Proof of the success of the railcars came with their substitution for locomotive-and-stock formations on this route. Further orders followed, the railcars being deployed on branch lines, their twin engines permitting trailing vehicles to be towed. Finally,

a variation of the design was introduced to serve as a parcels unit. Eventually 38 railcars of this basic design were built.

Some differences in the engines and transmissions inevitably occurred, though minor. All had a five-speed preselective Wilson epicyclic gearbox, but the final-drive ratios differed, according as a top speed of 75mph or extra torque for towing was required. The engines and gearboxes were connected through a Daimler fluid flywheel, manufactured under licence by AEC. Again, the drive train was mounted underfloor. The Western Region report concluded favourably on the use of railcars and their continued development.

Compared to these tentative steps down the diesel-railcar path in Britain, the pace of progress on the Continent, in particular on Germany's Reichsbahn (State Railways), was much faster. Attention naturally focused on the so-called 'Flying Hamburger' trains that plied between Berlin and Hamburg. By May 1933 these two-car units had stolen from the GWR's steam-hauled 'Cheltenham Flyer' the mantle of the world's fastest train, achieving an average of 77.4mph. Each car was powered by a Maybach quick-running engine of 410hp, coupled to an electric transmission.

Above: A typical Deutsche Reichsbahn (German State Railways) railcar of the 1930s. Some of these ran at speeds of up to 100mph.
Ian Allan Library

Right: The first rail application of hydraulic drive came in 1932 for a series of railbuses which were used in Austria and Poland. This photograph of an Austro-Daimler railbus is believed to have been taken at Innsbruck in March 1933. *Voith*

The LNER CME, Sir Nigel Gresley, is said to have considered acquiring one for trial, but its inability to put up a similar average between London and Newcastle, due to grade and speed restrictions, led him instead to design the famous 'A4' Pacific steam locomotives.

J. M. Voith Maschinenfabrik of Heidenheim had begun developing hydrodynamic power transmissions in 1929, in collaboration with Hermann Föttinger, the inventor of the hydrodynamic torque-converter and the hydrodynamic coupling. The evolution of a hydrodynamic multi-circuit transmission for rail application began in 1930. An important element in the development, which made the Voith converter suitable for rail application, was the use within the drive train of a Vulcan-Sinclair fluid coupling, which by 1932 was being used in other rail traction and industrial applications. Voith acquired the German and Austrian rights to this coupling.

The first installation came in 1932 in an Austro-Daimler railbus, with a Voith ABL 2.881 turbo-transmission and a fluid coupling close-coupled to an 80hp petrol engine of 3,000rpm. By early 1934 more than 60 of these were in service, mainly in Austria and Poland, and had prompted Deutsche Reichsbahn (German State Railways) to order two further railcars in 1933 to expand the 'Hamburger' service and for use elsewhere. The key difference from the first 'Hamburgers' was the use of a Voith hydraulic transmission.

By 1935 Voith transmissions were being used in railcars running at 100mph. In fact the 1930s witnessed a rapid expansion of diesel railcar production in Germany, with diesel-mechanical and (to a limited extent) diesel-hydraulic transmission both used as well as the diesel-electric traction system installed in the early 'Hamburgers'. In fact the 'Hamburger' sets were merely the first of a number of high-speed diesel railcars to emerge on Germany's railways during the 1930s, with start-to-stop timings of up to 82mph.

In 1933 Sir W. G. Armstrong-Whitworth & Co (Engineers) Ltd built the first main-line diesel locomotive to run in the UK, seen here at the manufacturer's works. *Ian Allan Library*

Concurrently, the Munich-based Maschinenfabrik Augsburg-Nürnberg (MAN) began developing a 'V' engine, then rated at 420hp but which was the progenitor of its L12V18/21 unit that was to see service in the Western Region's diesel-hydraulic locomotives of the 1950s and '60s.

Two points are now relevant to cover. First, by the beginning of the 1930s, the technical development of the diesel engine had reached the stage at which it had become a viable alternative to the petrol engine. Although the petrol engine was lighter for any given horsepower, weight was not as important an issue in rail applications as it was for road vehicles. At least one terrible accident involving a petrol railcar, in Italy in 1934, showed the danger of using such a volatile fuel in the railway environment. Secondly, despite the great promise of the above developments in diesel railcars, Britain had plentiful stocks of cheap coal at the time, and capital costs also favoured steam-powered railcars. These issues of economics continued into the 1950s and saw Britain in the rearguard in the replacement of steam traction.

Locomotives in Britain, Germany and the USA

Turning now to locomotives, the honour of being the first British main-line diesel example went to an unnumbered product built by Sir W. G. Armstrong-Whitworth & Co (Engineers) Ltd. This prototype was built in Newcastle in 1933 as a speculative venture and offered to the LNER for trials. The 1Co1 wheel arrangement was adopted. Power came from an Armstrong-Sulzer 8LD28 diesel of 800hp at 700rpm; this was the first main-line use in Britain of the Sulzer power plant that was to form the backbone of British Railways' diesel fleet from the 1950s until the 1980s. The engine drove an electric transmission system, but the pioneer proved short-lived, because it was not repaired after an engine crankcase explosion in April 1934. A lack of interest in diesel traction in Britain resulted in Armstrong-Whitworth's withdrawing from the market.

The first application of diesel-hydraulic transmission in a main-line locomotive was reported in the *Railway Gazette* on 24 January 1936. This locomotive was a design on trial in Germany; it had a 2-6-2 wheel arrangement (1-C-1 in UIC notation), which meant that the driving axles were coupled, whereas a 'Co' arrangement has three uncoupled driving axles. The locomotive was powered by a MAN turbocharged diesel of 1,250hp continuous (1,400hp for one hour) at 700rpm, and a Voith hydraulic transmission was used. Krauss-Maffei was the builder, and the locomotive had been exhibited at an event in Nuremberg to mark the 100th anniversary of the German Railways on 13 July 1935. Only one torque-converter was

The world's first main-line diesel-hydraulic locomotive, the Krauss-Maffei 1C1 (2-6-2 in Whyte notation) powered by a MAN turbocharged diesel of 1,250hp and driven through a Voith hydraulic transmission. It ran on the Prussian State Railway from 1935, bearing the number V140.001. *Voith*

fitted, but there were two hydraulic couplings, which gave a three-speed transmission. Although the decision to bolt the transmission directly to the locomotive's frames was not a success, because flexing of the frames distorted the transmission, No V140 001 remained the largest in the world up to the withdrawal of the locomotive in 1957.

Between 1934 and 1938 Maybach and Voith collaborated in the provision of complete powertrains. The arrangement ended when Maybach developed the Mekydro transmission, which was first applied in late 1938. Whereas Voith continued to follow Föttinger's principle of emptying-and-filling torque-converter chambers, the Mekydro was a disengageable permanently filled converter.

The Great Depression in the USA during the first half of the 1930s impacted on rail-borne passenger and freight traffic. The Chicago, Burlington & Quincy Railroad expressed interest to the Budd Corporation in the production of a promotional trainset for rail passenger travel. The result was the 'Burlington Zephyr', a streamlined three-car train with 72 seats and compartments for baggage and express freight. Built in April 1934, it had a Winton (General Motors) 8-201-A eight-cylinder diesel of 600hp, which powered an electric generator and traction motors. On 26 May a demonstration run between Denver and Chicago — a distance

of 1,015 miles — was made at an average of 77mph, with a top speed of 112½mph. Production versions soon followed.

A decade earlier, the Electro Motive Co began building railcars, using Winton Engine Co engines. In 1930 General Motors bought both these companies, and eventually they became the Electro Motive Division (EMD). Though by no means the inaugural EMD locomotive, the 'E' unit of 1937 was the first of a lineage of passenger locomotives that became the most numerous in the USA. Initially, it had a Winton 16-cylinder 201-A engine of 1,300hp, but from September 1938 a 16-cylinder 1,350hp variant of GM's new 567 range of engines was substituted. Working on a two-stroke cycle (whereas virtually all other diesels used in rail traction operate on a four-stroke cycle), this power unit was developed during the 1950s into the 645 model that eventually saw service in the British Railways Class 59 and the 710 model in Class 66.

It was in the field of freight traction, however, that American railways were most interested because it was much more lucrative than their passenger services, which were only marginally profitable. Large parts of the USA away from the eastern seaboard faced issues over consistent water supply, and the ability to change from water-hungry steam power to a diesel alternative was an attractive proposition. GM produced a demonstrator 'F' unit that attracted considerable interest and entered series production from 1939. The 'F' was a master-and-slave unit with a single driving cab; master and slave each had a 16-cylinder 1,350hp engine. Pairs of 'Fs' were frequently coupled back-to-back, to give a unit with a cab at each end and a combined power of 5,400hp.

Both the 'E' and 'F' series had diesel-electric drive, and were instrumental in the rapid decline of steam traction in the USA. Volume production from 1939, by GM in particular, kept unit costs low and made the company (and other US diesel locomotive manufacturers) highly competitive in world markets. Although alternatives to diesel-electric transmission were tried by these American companies, it was the concentration on this type of transmission that helped make it pre-eminent across the world for main-line locomotives.

The foregoing summarises the key developments that were to have a bearing on events after World War 2 in Britain. Whereas diesel traction was becoming accepted as advantageous for shunting locomotives, the case for its use on the main line was not yet seen as proven.

A General Motors 'F'-class locomotive, comprising 'master' and 'slave' units, each with a 1,350hp engine, heads the Southern Pacific 'Daylight' towards Santa Barbara, California.
B. A. Butt

2

DIESEL-ELECTRIC DEVELOPMENT AFTER 1945

LMS designs

In its 9 November 1945 issue the *Railway Gazette* referred to an announcement carried the previous month concerning an order secured by English Electric for 27 locomotives for Egyptian State Railways. Several months later came a further order for 19 complete diesel-electric trains for Egypt. Fifteen of the locomotives were 350hp shunters, based on the design already supplied to the LMS, LNER and SR.

The remaining 12 locomotives were described as to be general-purpose main-line locomotives of 1,600hp, with a design weight of 116 tons and mounted on two three-axle bogies, all axles being powered; there was to be a driving position at each side of the cab. Delivery of the locomotives began in late 1946. English Electric subcontracted the design of the mechanical parts to the Vulcan Foundry, which built six locomotives. In the event, in order to achieve the stipulated maximum axle load of 17 tons, a curious 1A-Do-A1 wheel arrangement was adopted to carry the 124-ton overall weight. English Electric used a 16-cylinder version of its SVT diesel engine, rated at 1,600hp at 750rpm. This engine was a development of the manufacturer's 'RK' range that had been used in shunting locomotives.

C. E. Fairburn, formerly of English Electric, had joined the LMS as Chief Electrical Engineer during 1934, and became CME during 1941. His principal assistant, H. G. Ivatt, was keen to examine the potential for main-line diesel traction, whereas, reputedly, R. C. Bond was not. The LMS did not develop any proposals for a main-line diesel locomotive before the outbreak of World War 2.

Immediately after the war Fairburn gave some consideration to a diesel-electric unit for mixed traffic, comparable with those of a 2-6-4 steam tank engine, a ghostly forerunner of the Type 2 locomotives that emerged as part of the Pilot Scheme to be described in Chapter 7. The project did not develop beyond discussions of the concept with British Thomson-Houston (BTH) in which a 1,500hp Paxman engine was envisaged.

Shortly after these discussions, in late 1945, a party of officers from the LMS (including E. S. Cox) and LNER (including A. H. Peppercorn) went to the USA. From this visit — and with Ivatt having succeeded Fairburn in January 1946 — emerged the design of 1,600hp diesel-electric locomotives Nos 10000 and 10001 and 800hp locomotive No 10800. Although the LMS had preliminary discussions with BTH and Crompton Parkinson, it was decided to collaborate with English Electric, possibly because English Electric was producing similar locomotives for Egypt, possibly because of joint experience with the diesel shunters, or possibly because the LMS and English Electric operated a 12-month exchange programme for works personnel. The collaboration was referred to as a joint venture, rather than the LMS having sole ownership of the project.

On 20 May 1946 the LMS and English Electric agreed in principle to produce a twin-unit traction set of 3,200hp, comprising two 1,600hp diesel locomotives. This was a refinement of the GM 'F' unit, which (as described in the previous chapter) was a single-cab master-and-slave formation that gave a combined 2,700hp, or 5,400hp if two such sets were coupled back-to-back. By contrast with the GM product, the LMS/English Electric design would be able to function as two separate 1,600hp locomotives of roughly power classification 5. Project costs were to be split; the LMS would design and build the mechanical parts, while English Electric would (at its own cost) supply the engine and electrical machines. History records that Ivatt drove No 10000 out of Derby Works on 8 December 1947, so it was an LMS locomotive, but only just! No 10001 was taken into stock during July 1948.

English Electric naturally opted for the 16SVT diesel engine that was to be fitted to its order from Egypt, with a rating of 1,600hp at 750rpm. The main generator was an EE823A,

The LMS copied American practice by conceiving of Nos 10000 and 10001 as a single unit, in order to match the performance of an '8P' Pacific. Taken on 5 October 1948, this photograph shows the pair about to depart with the 1pm Glasgow train, which they would work as far as Carlisle. *Ian Allan Library*

and there were six four-pole EE519/3B traction motors. The weight in working order was 130.6 tons, the top speed was 90mph, and the maximum tractive effort was given as 41,400lb. A three-axle, double-bogie arrangement, with all axles powered, was selected, and the ride quality, although 'springy', was very good.

Nos 10000 and 10001 entered revenue-earning service during February and July 1948 respectively; British Railways classified them both as '5MT'. During the late 1940s, official records refer to these two machines as one traction unit, which points to an intention to use them regularly in multiple, replicating American practice, so there is no question but that the pair was capable of timing any contemporary service booked for the most powerful LMR Pacifics. Although most of the running during the early years was along the West Coast main line, with allocation to either London Camden or Willesden sheds, some duties were performed on the Midland route out of St Pancras. Steam generators for train heating proved unreliable, so the duo was put on freight services singly during the winter,

returning to passenger work as a pair in more clement weather.

Cecil J. Allen's articles on locomotive practice and performance as published in *The Railway Magazine* offer useful insights into contemporary operation, and the September 1949 issue was devoted entirely to the duo. Referred to by the writer as a 'twin-unit' (suggesting continuity of the concept of a single traction unit), they had recently entered traffic between London and Glasgow, making a daily return run of over 800 miles. While Allen acknowledged this as remarkable from a British standpoint he observed that 700-ton trains between Chicago and Denver (1,048 miles) were timed in as little as 15½ hours, while the Denver–Omaha leg of 560 miles was timed to produce an average speed of 73.8mph, including seven stops. By contrast the 'Royal Scot' of the summer of 1949 was booked for 8hr 25min northbound, as against the prewar schedule of seven hours with a 420-ton load, these timings being based on the use of an LMS Pacific. Allen estimated that the 'twin unit' could keep to the prewar time with a 520-ton train.

Two points of particular interest can be gleaned from the article. First, the locomotives had an eight-notch power controller, and a control system that enabled full power to be obtained by progressively opening up over only 15 seconds. The other point concerns the performance up Shap and Beattock. After climbing Shap from a check through Tebay, the speed was 32mph at the summit. The generous schedule meant that, approaching Beattock station, the speed had been allowed to drift below 40mph, though in preparation for the stiff climb the effort was stepped up to 51mph at the start. Again the minimum was 32mph. Although rolling resistance values for prewar carriages are not to hand, modern values for stock of lower resistance will suffice for speeds in the 30-40mph band. On both climbs, rhp values of around 2,350 were produced,[†] and, allowing for a slight underestimate of train resistance, it is evident that the locomotives were delivering their rated output of 2,500rhp combined, or 3,200 engine hp. On another journey with a 390-ton consist, unchecked between Carnforth and Shap Summit (passing speeds of 58 and 49mph) but with an easing round the Low Gill curves, the 31.4 miles

† *Rail horsepower (rhp) is the horsepower at the locomotive wheel rims, available to move the locomotive and train.*

were covered in an unprecedented 29min 50sec. The combined rail horsepower on Grayrigg was 2,560.

These performances proved that the pair could match the best running of the most powerful Pacifics, not just in short bursts as for steam, but throughout the whole London–Glasgow journey if necessary. Running on the Midland main line out of St Pancras also proved that either of the prototypes on its own could match '6P' steam running over long distances. Between 6 and 9 June 1951 No 10001 was put through trials between Euston and Glasgow on the 'Royal Scot', returning on an overnight service; loads were up to 517 tons tare. It was established that a single locomotive could time the trains.

Other trials on passenger work during this early period included the 'Bon Accord' (1.35pm Glasgow–Aberdeen). One contemporary editorial suggested that the 'twin unit' should be tried between Edinburgh and Aberdeen, where loads on the through services from London were very heavy and the route abounded in steep grades and sharp curves; nothing came of this. Trials on one of the LMR's premier freights were, however, conducted for an extended period during 1949/50. The 2.55pm Camden–Crewe was a fully fitted working, timed for a top speed of 53mph with a load of up to 45 wagons — roughly 515 tons but with a higher rolling

The LMS prototypes are seen here on 20 July 1950, passing through Tring on a diagram that covered the up 'Royal Scot' and a down overnight train. *BR*

Left: Unreliable train heating equipment kept the prototypes off winter passenger services. Here No 10001 is seen near Berkhamsted on 25 March 1950 with the 5.15am Edge Hill–Camden goods.
E. D. Bruton

Below: This time it is No 10000 that has been caught by the photographer, in charge of a freight at Rugby on 14 October 1950.
H. Weston

Right: Both the LMS prototypes spent time on the Southern in the company of their SR cousins. No 10000 heads the 'Bournemouth Belle' through Woking in April 1953. *J. M. Davenport*

resistance than passenger stock. Full details of the fuel used on this and the return journey were kept, and pointed to a fuel efficiency of 28-30%, whereas a modern steam locomotive returned about 8%. Despite this advantage the Railway Executive felt that continued investment in steam traction was justified.

By early 1952 Nos 10000 and 10001 had run a combined total of 600,000 miles, no mean achievement for prototype machines. In March/April 1953 the duo were transferred to the Southern Region's Nine Elms shed, where for almost two years they worked alongside the Southern diesel prototypes (of which more anon). On returning to the LMR, the locomotives appeared to be low on power, and first No 10001 went to Derby Works for examination. Adjustment of the fuel pumps remedied the situation, but the locomotive could not complete a Derby–St Pancras return run without being refuelled in London. After some argument, new fuel pumps and injectors were provided, and this resolved the low-power issue.

No 10800

At the same time as the 'twin-unit' described above was ordered the LMS also put in hand a design for a small diesel locomotive of power classification 3. It is possible to see American influence here too, because the layout resembled a 'road switcher', with a single cab, located slightly off-centre between the engine/main generator set and cooler group at one end and the control cubicle at the other. The resultant locomotive, No 10800, was built by NBL, though whether this was a collaborative project or a simple supply contract is not known.

Paxman's RPH model engine, in 16-cylinder configuration, was selected and provided 827hp at 1,250rpm. Coupled to it was a British Thomson-Houston (BTH) main generator, accompanied by a BTH auxiliary generator. Four BTH traction motors were axle-hung on the Bo-Bo bogies. Overall weight was just under 70 tons. The top speed was 70mph and the maximum tractive effort was 34,500lb.

No 10800 was delivered from NBL to Polmadie shed in May 1950 and was formally taken into stock on 1 July. A four-coach special was run between Euston and Watford on 14 November, with a top speed of 69.8mph. Although its initial allocation was to Willesden shed, the locomotive was tried on a range of work —

Below: No 10800, the LMS prototype built by NBL, in as-built condition. *BR*

quite natural for a prototype — which involved its being based at Bletchley for duties including freights to Oxford. During 1952 some time was spent working between Derby and Manchester Central, where it appears to have been used on passenger services that were beyond its very modest installed power.

From July 1952 it was lent to the Southern Region (official records refer to ownership resting with the London Midland Region, unlike Nos 10000 and 10001, which were 'transferred' from the LMR to the SR). Again a range of work was assigned. A lot of time was spent out of traffic, first for an intermediate overhaul and then after a major engine failure. Returning to traffic on 11 December 1954, No 10800 was lent to the neighbouring Plaistow shed on the Eastern Region. Here it was tried out on trip and short freight duties on the former North London Railway and London, Tilbury & Southend Railway routes; some passenger turns were also worked over the latter's metals. Although this was often described as an unsuccessful trial, the 1955 Pilot Scheme orders (see Chapter 7) included two designs of 800hp locomotives for precisely this work.

From February 1955 No 10800 was based mainly at Rugby, where it remained until a further classified repair was due, which brought about its withdrawal from traffic in April 1959 and from stock four months later.

The Southern Railway prototypes

In the same year that the LMS authorised Nos 10000 and 10001 the Southern embarked on a similar project, which culminated in the production of Nos 10201 and 10202. The Southern had considerable experience of electric traction by then, and no doubt the design work of the diesel-electric prototypes was a collaboration between O. V. S. Bulleid (CME) and C. M. Cock (CEE). All three were assigned HOO Lot No 3441, dated 22 February 1947.

Several fundamental changes from the LMS design were made. Most important was the bogie, which had four axles, three of them powered and the leading one unpowered. This lowered the maximum axle weight but pushed up overall weight. By way of explanation, the

Southern had learned that small-wheeled bogies, with traction motors that were nose-suspended and axle-hung, were punishing on the permanent way. The four-axle bogie arrangement arose as a consequence of a need to reduce the ratio of axle weight in tons to wheel diameter in feet, or P/D, to a figure not exceeding 4.5. This ratio was fixed by the Chief Civil Engineer in order to control excessive rail breakage, as a high P/D ratio was thought at that time to be one of the main contributory causes of fractured rails. An 18-ton axle load limit also offered a wide route availability.

Whereas the LMS had followed American practice in providing a nose end to the cab front, to avoid 'sleeper flutter', the Southern had not found this to be a problem with its

Top: No 10800 was sent to the SR for evaluation, but spent much of the time out of traffic undergoing an overhaul. It is seen at Norwood Junction during April 1953. *F. J. Saunders*

Above: No 10800 at Derby after its withdrawal, 1959. *Richard Lewis / Rail Photoprints*

EMUs, so a flat cab front was chosen. The LMS had incorporated cab-front doors to permit crews to pass between Nos 10000 and 10001 when working in multiple, but the Southern saw no need for this facility.

The choice of power equipment was, again, English Electric; but by the time the 16SVT diesels were delivered, the rating had been pushed up to 1,750hp at 750rpm, partly by the substitution of Napier turbochargers for the previous Brown Boveri type. This was only a one-hour rating, however: 1,600hp remained the continuous figure. The English Electric traction motors were type 519/4D. The gearing was 52:21, to permit a top speed of 110mph, but this was not found to be appropriate, and a lower ratio of 65:17 was fitted after a couple of years. This brought the

continuous rating speed down from 37 to 21½mph and raised the top speed to 85mph, the Southern Region line limit; the maximum tractive effort changed in consequence from 31,200 to 48,000lb. A progressive feature was the use of dry-pack engine room filters, in place of the usual oil-wetted type. The overall weight was 135 tons.

Construction of No 10201 started at Ashford Works during the summer of 1949. The locomotive record card gives a completion date of 30 December 1950 and initial allocation to Derby; costs were apportioned at £33,827 for the mechanical parts and £43,178 for the power equipment, a total of £77,005.

Trial running began in December 1950 on the Southern, and then for a couple of weeks

during January 1951 on the LMR out of St Pancras. On the LMR the 1-in-100 grades through the Peak District proved too severe for the high traction-motor gearing. Cecil J. Allen was able to describe two runs behind No 10201 as early as his March 1951 article in *The Railway Magazine*. Both were on an up express from Derby, which made seven intermediate calls before St Pancras; the load was the customary nine carriages. Schedule time was kept without difficulty, and speeds of 58 to 60mph were achieved on the 1-in-200 climbs, fully up to the 1,750hp rating. Allen's only adverse remark was that the locomotive was slow getting away from stops, no doubt owing to the high gear ratio and high continuous rating, requiring a more circumspect opening-up of power.

After exhibition at the Festival of Britain for virtually all of 1951, No 10201 began its service life at Eastleigh shed, moving to Nine Elms in 1953. No 10202 also was built at Ashford, construction being completed on 15 September 1951. No 10202 went into regular service on 15 October 1951, its first duty being on the 1.00pm Waterloo–Exeter Central, returning to Waterloo on the 5.55pm from Exeter, and on 29 October it began full scheduled working on the West of England main line, which included the 1.25am to Exeter and the 7.30am to Waterloo. Early in 1952 it joined No 10201 at Eastleigh shed. After their transfer to the LMR, Nos 10201 and 10202 were derated to 1,600hp on 19 August and 16 November 1956 respectively.

The third prototype, No 10203, was built at Brighton, and had the same design of mechanical parts as the earlier two. By now English Electric was able to offer its 16SVT diesel at a rating of 2,000hp at 850rpm. The traction motors were of type EE526A. With gearing for an 85mph top speed, the maximum tractive effort was 50,000lb; the overall weight was 132 tons; and the cost was £33,757 for the mechanical parts and £53,328 for the power equipment, amounting to £87,085 in total. The record card gives the completion date as 30 April 1954. No 10203 was allocated to Nine Elms shed along with the four other large diesel prototypes.

Nos 10202 and 10203 were put through dynamometer trials on the Southern Region. No 10202 had the higher traction motor gearing at the time, while No 10203 had run over 100,000 miles by the start of the trials in June 1955 and was found to be delivering a brake horsepower of only 1,883, as opposed to the intended 2,000. The following table shows the tractive-effort figures in pounds, with an unrebuilt SR 'Merchant Navy' Pacific for comparison.

Speed (mph)	Tractive effort (lb)		
	No 10202	**No 10203**	**Steam**
30	17,000	18,000	19,000
50	9,000	10,500	12,000
70	5,000	6,600	8,000
80	3,000	4,500	6,000

On the basis of the trials, the Western Region calculated that No 10203 could achieve a timing of 163 minutes for the 173.8 miles between Paddington and Exeter, as compared with 169½ minutes for the WR's 'King' 4-6-0. No 10203 was found to burn the same quantity of fuel as No 10000, demonstrating the improved efficiency of the engine after some seven years of development.

Official reports on operational experience

As part of the deliberations in the lead-up to the placing of Pilot Scheme orders the

No 10203 was the most powerful of the Southern prototypes, and was put through road trials shortly after being built. This view at Andover on 19 July 1954 features it in charge of a service train but with the Western Region dynamometer car as the leading vehicle. *G. Wheeler*

following year, a report dated 15 September 1954 described the performance of the five main-line diesel-electric locomotives then in service on the Southern Region. Of course, No 10203 had entered service only shortly before the report was produced. During the period covered by the report, weekly diagrams were assigned that amounted to 16,750 miles per week. During one weekday a locomotive was taken for servicing, which absorbed up to 12 hours but left all five machines available at weekends. Intermediate engine overhauls were carried out after 5,000 engine hours, corresponding to 150,000 miles, at which interval the electrical machines received a thorough check and the tyres were turned. Fuelling was done daily at Waterloo, and the locomotives inspected at the same time. Although the intervals differed, this maintenance regime was clearly the precursor of the one used by British Railways for its diesel fleet during the 1960s.

Of note is the specific reference to the lack of deterioration in locomotive performance as the date for an overhaul approached, which was the tendency that steam locomotives displayed, requiring the assignment of lighter duties, and the diesels' performance was not dependent on the skill of the train crew, as was the case with steam.

As against a theoretical availability of 6½ days per week, during 1954 up to 17 July, the actual availability was only 44%. This was because No 10000 was out of traffic for 120 days for the replacement of a cracked cylinder block, while No 10201 was stopped for an intermediate overhaul, which included modifications to the exhausters, fire-fighting equipment and traction motors. Adjusting for these events, availability would have been 60%. The report cites miles run for six four-weekly periods up to 27 March 1954, which coincided with the general overhauls of both No 10000 and No 10001. No 10201 ran 51,315 miles, and No 10202 47,312 miles.

The duties performed were mainly working Class 1 passenger trains between Waterloo and Exeter Central or Waterloo to Bournemouth Central and Weymouth; these included overnight services. There was one freight turn, up from Exmouth to Nine Elms, and a milk train between Templecombe and Clapham Junction. For the whole of 1953, the ex-LMS examples ran 46,659 miles after allocation to the Southern Region, while Nos 10201 and 10202 managed 95,837. Weekdays in and out of service for any reason were as follows:

	In service	Out of service
Nos 10000 and 10001 (LMS)	103½	211½
Nos 10201 and 10202 (SR)	178½	136½

Availability was therefore 33% for the LMS locomotives and 57% for the Southern pair. Performance for 1954 up to 17 July was similar.

Interestingly, figures for No 10800 are included in the reports, because the locomotive was working on the Southern Region during 1953. The region seems to have been caught at a time when the locomotive was due for a classified overhaul, because 160 weekdays were lost for this reason, and contributed to an availability of only 28% and a total of only 24,975 miles run. The classified overhaul again had a marked impact during the first half of 1954, with an availability of only 18%.

In April 1956 a report was produced that dealt with all of the seven main-line diesel locomotives then allocated to the LMR. The period covered operational experience between transfers from the Southern Region, starting in March 1955 and 28 January 1956, or a shorter

Some time after all five main-line diesels had been transferred to the LMR, No 10201 hurries a Birmingham–Euston working past Bourne End on 30 July 1955. *Philip J. Kelley*

Left: No 10203 while on loan to the London Midland Region c1955. *Ian Allan Library*

Left: No 10203 heads an up freight near Tring on 24 March 1959. *S. J. Jefferson*

period if the relevant locomotive was not in traffic on the LMR in March 1955. Nos 10000, 10001, 10201 and 10202 were all rated at 1,750hp, and the duties assigned to the quartet, plus No 10203, comprised Euston to Bletchley, Liverpool and Manchester, the LMS duo also working to Carlisle, Nos 10201 and 10202 working to Wolverhampton, and No 10203 going as far as Glasgow. No 10800 was operating between Peterborough, Birmingham and Leicester, including Weedon–Market Harborough freights while based at Rugby, and local freights between Poplar, St Pancras and Willesden while at Devons Road shed.

During the period of the report, the availability of the large locomotives varied from 44% (No 10001) to 66% (No 10000); No 10800 achieved 60%, and the average for all six was 55%. Analysis of the faults attributed 56% to design and manufacturing issues, 32% to depot maintenance issues and 12% due to operating department issues. The six-pole traction motors fitted to No 10203 were more prone to flashover than the four-pole machines used in the earlier large diesels. These motors also got through motor brushes at a high rate, the commutators being likened to razor blades.

Explaining the low availability, 62% of the time in Derby Works and 6% of depot time was due to awaiting materials, and the lost time was judged to have pulled availability down from a potential 65-70%, if spares had been on hand. By contrast, steam locomotive availability was quoted as 80%. There was no mention of the lack of appropriate maintenance facilities at running sheds.

The conclusions reached were expressed in terms of the prospects for the future of the orders placed in 1955 under the Pilot Scheme, and included the view that the experience gained would assist manufacturers with Pilot Scheme designs and help planning for large-scale diesel operation. The number of locomotives, which were admitted to be prototypes, was small, and this impacted on staff familiarity and the viability of holding spares.

In good years, over 110,000 miles could be run, while No 10202 managed 149,122 during 1957, a figure equalled only by a very select few of British Railways' standard types. Such achievements cannot be judged as anything other than a success. As the 1950s drew to a close, and increasing numbers of new Type 4s came on stream, interest in the non-standard prototypes waned, and all were withdrawn during the period 1958-66.

A 'Deltic' diversion

On 20 November 1951 an internal order was generated within English Electric for the production of a locomotive of an entirely new design that was aimed at both home and overseas markets. This was to have a profound effect on the British railway scene over the next 30 years.

During 1947 an English Electric subsidiary, D. Napier & Sons Ltd of Liverpool, had developed a high-speed engine for the Royal Navy, which was of the opposed-piston configuration and named the 'Deltic'. Commentators differ as to the origin of the possible application of this engine for rail traction, but there is agreement that the result was an entirely English-Electric-inspired private venture, the aim being to construct a prototype locomotive of very high power yet with a wide route availability; this locomotive received the name *Deltic*.

For rail applications the 18-cylinder D18-25 engine was rated to produce 1,650hp at 1,500rpm. The engine design was also lightweight, two units, delivering 3,300hp, together weighing roughly half as much as a single English Electric 16SVT, then rated at 1,750hp. In the new locomotive two of these engines were fitted; each drove an EE831A main generator, each of which supplied power to three EE526A traction motors. This was the same motor as used in No 10203, and the same 61:19 gearing was used. During early service operation it quickly emerged that this ratio was too low for a locomotive of such power, so the ratio was revised to 59:21.

English Electric calculated the maximum tractive effort to be 52,500lb and the

On 28 August 1956 *Deltic* leaves Skipton whilst on test over the Settle & Carlisle line. *S. D. Widd*

continuous rating at the original gearing 29,000lb at 35mph, yielding 2,700rhp. Concerned about the risk that so powerful a traction unit might cause drawbar failures in its train, especially during surges when wheelslip was encountered, English Electric sought to limit the maximum tractive effort by causing the main generator to trip out at 2,700A. At low speed, tractive effort is directly proportional to main generator current. No doubt in conjunction with the BTC, a safe maximum of 48,000lb was settled on when deciding the upper limit on generator current for service use; in other words, the generator would trip and prevent the driver from achieving a tractive effort higher than 48,000lb.

All this was built into a traditional form of mechanical parts and mounted on two Co bogies. For an overall weight of 106 tons, this prototype was considerably more powerful than anything else running in Britain at the time; for more than five years, indeed, it was the most powerful single-unit diesel locomotive in the world.

A special meeting of the BTC Technical Research & Development Committee took place on 8 December 1954 to discuss the private venture by English Electric, involving the construction of a 3,300hp locomotive. The BTC's Engineering Officer and Committee chairman, J. C. L. Train (who was also

chairman of the Works & Equipment Committee), and representatives of the Central Staff had visited English Electric's works at both Liverpool and Preston, where the prototype *Deltic* was under construction and where the engines that gave it its name were built. The committee agreed that the locomotive could be used on British Railways, initially on freight services on the LMR and then on London–Glasgow passenger duties, while it should be put through a detailed series of trials under BTC control.

The minutes are clear that the Committee was keen on the prospect of the use of Deltic engines, but it is not recorded whether this was because they offered a high power-to-weight ratio like the German MAN and Maybach variants. Noting that the Works & Equipment Committee had already approved proposals for 160 main-line diesel-electric locomotives of designs to be agreed, the Technical Committee suggested that 10 of them should incorporate a nine-cylinder Deltic engine, turbocharged to deliver 1,250hp; in fact, the actual rating was 1,100hp.

A meeting of the Works & Equipment Committee on 7 September 1955 gave approval to the draft agreement for granting facilities to English Electric for *Deltic*'s operation on British Railways. This set the scene for the locomotive to take to British

English Electric prototype *Deltic* was the world's most powerful single-unit diesel from its construction until 1962. Here it is seen as prepared for exhibition in the Science Museum after its withdrawal. *John F. Hughes*

Railways metals the following month, based at Liverpool Edge Hill shed, in order to be close to Napier's factory. The Works & Equipment Committee laid down initial diagramming on freight services because it was appreciated that no contemporary passenger duty could make use of the installed power.

During August and September 1956 *Deltic* was rigged up and put through a full series of dynamometer car trials over the Settle & Carlisle line. Although this route presented taxing gradients, the overall line speed at the time was only 60mph, thus limiting the extent of high-speed testing.

The trials established the total engine output as 3,250hp, against 3,300hp theoretical; this was within the normal tolerance. The rail horsepower was found to be a little below the predicted values, but was still astounding for a diesel locomotive of the time, and consistent across the speed range over which full power could be applied continuously. The following table gives sample values.

Rail horsepower achieved by *Deltic* on trial

Speed (mph)	Rail horsepower
20	2,380
30	2,580
40	2,650
60	2,650
80	2,630
90	2,620

Transmission losses — the power lost between the engine output shaft and the wheelsl — were estimated as 6% in the main generators, 8% in the traction motors and 5% in the auxiliary equipment. Subtracting these losses gives a transmission efficiency of 81%, which can be judged to be good. The maximum tractive effort was recorded as 45,500lb — very close to the 48,000lb calculated limit set by English Electric via the main generator overload trips. This corresponded to just 19% of the locomotive's total weight (or its adhesion factor). It should

have meant that *Deltic* was less prone to slipping, because its maximum potential tractive effort for the installed power was not exploited. On the basis of the trials, it was calculated that the locomotive would be able to ascend Shap with a 500-ton train at no less than 41mph.

By the time *Deltic* moved to the Eastern Region in January 1959 the decision to acquire a fleet of 22 similar machines for London–Edinburgh duties had already been taken. The LMR was not interested in such a powerful traction unit, by reason of the sanctioning of electrification for the West Coast route out of London to the West Midlands and the North West. By contrast the East Coast Main Line Area Board appreciated that electrification was no longer an option in the foreseeable future, but in order to accelerate passenger services along this artery, something beyond what was planned in the Pilot Scheme would be needed, and the English Electric prototype fitted the bill.

The production units were to prove the most powerful class of diesels to run on British Railways for 30 years. Being something of a blind alley within the story being told in this book, that part in it played by the 'Deltics' will be concluded here. In a sense both those who supported and those who opposed the acquisition of the production 'Deltics' were right. The operators saw the high installed power as essential for the train service they knew they needed to provide in order to compete with air travel. Conversely, elements of the mechanical engineering side were opposed, because the engines appeared to be rather complex pieces of equipment and likely to be expensive to maintain. From the late 1970s, by which time the HST sets were in regular service on the East Coast, the 'Deltic' fleet was quickly phased out, being deemed too expensive and too complex to be deployed elsewhere. Nevertheless, the performance of *Deltic* back in 1956 had demonstrated to British Railways the benefits that could be derived from the use of quick-running engines in facilitating a single traction unit of very high power.

Right: The Napier Deltic engines could be smoky when opened up after a period of idling. No 9011 *The Royal Northumberland Fusiliers* proves the point as it leaves Edinburgh Waverley for London on 3 June 1972 heading the up 'Talisman'. *J. H. Cooper-Smith*

3

GAS-TURBINE PROPULSION

No 18000

Early in 1946 F. W. Hawksworth, CME of the Great Western Railway, examined the world's first gas-turbine locomotive, which had been ordered in 1939 and delivered in 1941 by Brown Boveri in Switzerland. During the following October, the GWR ordered No 18000 from British Brown-Boveri Ltd. It was constructed by Brown Boveri, Baden, Switzerland, in conjunction with the Swiss Locomotive and Machine Works (SLM) at Winterthur, which was responsible for the mechanical parts, comprising, essentially, the bogies, the mainframe and the superstructure.

No 18000's turbine developed around 10,300hp at 5,300rpm, of which 7,800hp was required to power the compressor, leaving 2,500hp to drive the main generator, which had a continuous rating of 1580kW. A Saurer diesel engine was coupled to a 10kW auxiliary generator, which supplied all the auxiliaries as well as power for starting the turbine. It developed sufficient power to drive two traction motors for light-engine movements at up to 15mph.

The traditional arrangement in diesel-electric locomotives had generally been to have nose-suspended traction motors, but this causes a high unsprung weight on the axle and has an adverse effect on the track. By contrast, the Brown Boveri arrangement, which used an individual axle drive with a quill stump and spring coupling, achieved a considerable reduction in the unsprung weight, because the motor and gear were fixed rigidly to the bogie frame. The four motors were connected in an all-parallel arrangement; each had an output of 420hp, 585A, 720V at 1,550rpm.

To achieve an acceptable maximum axle loading, the locomotive was mounted on two three-axle bogies. The outer axles on each bogie were each powered by one of the four traction motors. Gearing was for a top speed of 90mph, and the predicted maximum tractive effort was 31,500lb, with a continuous tractive effort of 12,400lb at 64mph (2,100rhp). A British Railways publication describing the locomotive gives the overall weight as 115 tons, but other sources quote different values.

Study of the accompanying diagrams will reveal how this form of traction works. A single-stage open-cycle gas turbine (B), with the heat-exchanger (D), was used for the power unit. The air was aspirated by the compressor (C), compressed and passed through the heat-exchanger, where it was preheated and delivered to the combustion chamber (A). Unlike the arrangement found in aircraft turbines, there was only a single combustion chamber. In the combustion chamber only part of the air was used for the combustion of the fuel oil injected under pressure, the remaining and by far the larger part serving to cool the side walls of the combustion chamber and to reduce the gas temperature at the turbine inlet (4) to the value determined by the heat-resisting qualities of the blade material and the long service life demanded of such a plant. The hot gases expanding in the gas turbine (B) produced mechanical work, part of which was used to drive the compressor (C), and the rest, forming the actual useful output, was transmitted to the main generator (F) through a reduction gear (E). Before escaping through roof louvres (6) to the atmosphere, the turbine exhaust gases passed through the heat-exchanger, giving up part of their heat to the compressed air on its way to the combustion chamber, which brought about a corresponding reduction in fuel consumption.

Outline diagram showing how a gas turbine works. *BR*

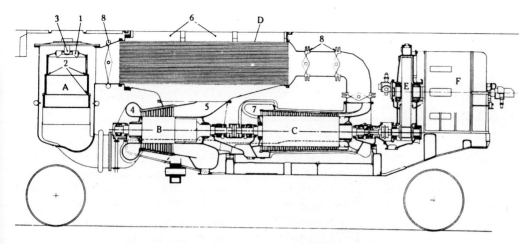

A. Combustion Chamber	1. Combustion Air Swirl Vanes
B. Gas Turbine	2. Secondary Air Inlets
C. Air Compressor	3. Burner Nozzle
D. Heat Exchanger	4. Turbine Inlet
E. Generator Reduction Gear	5. Turbine Exhaust
F. Generator	6. Exhaust louvres to atmosphere
	7. Compressor air inlet
	8. Expansion joints

FIG.7 - CROSS SECTION OF GAS TURBINE POWER UNIT

The air was taken in through openings symmetrically placed in either side wall of the locomotive and connected to the air intakes (7) of the compressor by two enclosed ducts. This was done in order to prevent the combustion air from mixing with oil vapour, or from becoming preheated in the machine room. Nevertheless, during No 18000's life several fires occurred in the heat-exchanger.

A large, handwheel type of power controller, a common arrangement on the Continent, acted on the governing system of the gas turbine and produced a preset output corresponding to each of several notches. The actual power produced was determined by the turbine speed and fuel flow rate. Although the detail of how the control system operated is outside the scope of this book, it is worth noting that the top two power controller notches did not increase power but initiated traction-motor field weakening to permit the highest possible road speed.

Whereas a diesel-electric locomotive simply has an ammeter registering the main generator current, for No 18000 Brown Boveri devised a cross-pointer instrument that the driver had to monitor. It simultaneously indicated the main generator current and

voltage and the tractive effort being developed by the locomotive. From the point of intersection of the two pointers, the driver was able to judge the appropriate moment for traction-motor field weakening.

Delivery of No 18000 was delayed by a wrangle between the Department of Transport and the Department of Trade over the payment of import duty. On arrival at Harwich, on 5 February 1950, the locomotive was towed to Swindon. A press trip from Paddington to Plymouth was arranged for

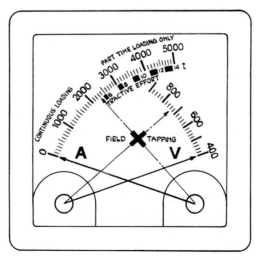

14 March, but was cancelled when a compressor blade failed five days previously during test running. Friday 19 May saw the first passenger train hauled, from Paddington to Swindon. Three days later No 18000 took up a regular diagram on the 3.30pm Paddington–Plymouth and 7.15am return.

Initial trials over the South Devon banks had shown that a 436-ton train could be taken out of Plymouth up the 1-in-42 Hemerdon Bank; a later trial established 297 tons as the limit when the train had to be restarted on the incline. Although this corresponded to the manufacturer's predicted performance curve, it was disappointing for the Operating Department, because this was a smaller limiting load than the limit of about 350 tons set for a 'King' steam locomotive. In those days, the fact that a locomotive of No 18000's power was incapable of matching a less powerful steam locomotive could not be readily appreciated, because experience with electrical machine design and gearing for railway application was still in its infancy, for traction units of this power.

The October 1950 issue of *The Railway Magazine* included a write-up by Cecil J. Allen of a run behind No 18000. The trailing load was 363 tons tare (385 tons gross) as far as Westbury, where the usual slip coach was detached just before the avoiding line at Heywood Road Junction. This easy schedule provided no opportunity for deployment of the full capabilities of this (for its time) powerful locomotive. As if to demonstrate this, after a maximum of 65mph through Slough, there was an easing of power, and the speed fell away to 57½mph on level track at Langley. Reading was therefore passed in 37 minutes.

Even climbing the Kennett Valley, No 18000 was not extended, and a further easing saw the speed drop to 33mph over Savernake Summit, and nothing higher than 71½mph was needed on the descent past Lavington to keep the train ahead of schedule. A sprint along the Langport cut-off line, saw the speed touch 80mph, with some good climbs over this undulating stretch. Despite an easy run in, Taunton was reached in 145min 17sec, nearly three minutes early, Allen estimating that 138 minutes would easily have been possible.

Climbing to Whiteball, the train was accelerated to 58½mph on gradients as steep as 1 in 174, below Wellington, where level track added 2mph to the speed. Against the 1 in 86 to 1 in 80 before Whiteball Tunnel mouth, the speed fell to 51mph, and then No 18000 was eased again to avoid the risk of slipping in the tunnel. This ascent beat by 55 seconds from the Taunton restart the best 'King' effort with a similar load known to Allen.

In line with No 18000's limitations over the South Devon banks, the load was reduced to only 215 tons at Exeter St Davids, so a full-load run over the South Devon banks was ruled out. After passing Newton Abbot at 35mph the train accelerated to around 50mph through Aller Junction, and to 60mph on the 1-in-90 lower part of Dainton Bank. The minimum at the summit was 41mph, producing a pass-to-pass time from Newton Abbot of 4min 56sec. After negotiating Totnes at 45mph the train slowed only briefly below 40mph as it climbed Rattery Bank. Despite a check outside North Road station, arrival at Plymouth was more than five minutes inside the 76min booking, leading Allen to conclude that No 18000 surpassed a 'King', the WR's most powerful steam type.

On another occasion during 1950, O. S. Nock travelled behind No 18000 on the up train from Plymouth, when the trailing load was also around 350 tons. Going all-out, the prototype topped Whiteball Summit at 60mph — a speed well below what a 2,500hp diesel-electric would have achieved with such a load.

September 1951 brought yet more dynamometer-car trials, this time between Paddington and Plymouth with a trailing load close to that on Allen's trip. Runs comparable to those of the Western Region's express steam locomotives were made, with a view to determining No 18000's overall fuel efficiency. This series of tests established fuel efficiencies of 6.6% for No 18000, 5.45% for 'Castle' No 5049 *Earl of Plymouth* and 5.36% for 'King' No 6022 *King Edward III*. Such a low efficiency value for the gas turbine was extremely disappointing and reflected the inherent issue that gas-turbine efficiency at that time fell sharply at load factors below 80%. The full-load efficiency had been established as 16.9%.

Other test results confirmed the maximum tractive effort as 30,000lb up to 20mph, and 8,800lb at 70mph, both corresponding to around 1,600hp at the rail. Indeed, the performance recorded by Allen referred to above was more in line with what a locomotive delivering around 1,600rhp would achieve, rather than the standard of a British Railways Class 45 of 2,500hp, which produced around 2,000rhp. Transmission efficiency was therefore only 64% for a turbine output of 2,500hp. The balancing speed on level track with a 400-ton load was 78mph, a rate in accord with 1,600rhp. Performance at this level is perhaps unsurprising when it is remembered that the traction motors had a combined output of only 1,680hp.

No 18100 (left) and No 18000 (right) inside the erecting shop at Swindon Works on 23 May 1953.
R. S. Wilkins / Rail Photoprints

No 18000 was nicknamed 'Kerosene Castle', no doubt because of its unmistakable oily exhaust. Allocated to Old Oak Common, the locomotive appears to have spent most of its operating life on workings between Paddington and Bristol. During 1958 complaints from track gangs about the fumes emitted as it passed through the Severn Tunnel resulted in its being barred. It received its last general overhaul at Swindon Works during December 1956, painting being completed on 8 January 1957, although its return to traffic was delayed until April by flashover damage in the traction motors. In 1959 damage caused by equipment left on the track was not repaired, although the locomotive was not withdrawn until 16 December 1960. At the time of writing, No 18000 survives as a preserved exhibit at Barrow Hill.

No 18100

Concurrent with the ordering of No 18000, on 11 September 1946, the GWR entered into an agreement with the Metropolitan-Vickers Electrical Co Ltd ('Metrovick') for the design, building, testing and operation of a gas-turbine locomotive, with the costs to be borne equally. The CME of the GWR set out the principal features, which were based on the service requirements, namely that the locomotive should be able to handle the GWR's heaviest passenger trains, particularly between London and Plymouth, at speeds of up to 90mph. Hence, to cope with the South Devon banks, a maximum starting tractive effort of 60,000lb and a continuous tractive effort of 30,000lb were required. To avoid exceeding the maximum axle loads two six-axle bogies were needed. A nominal output at the turbine shaft of 3,500hp was selected, and the design of the turbine, reduction gear and electric transmission equipment was based on that figure, although the blade profiles in this particular machine limited continuous output to between 3,100 and 3,200hp, the continuous rating being declared as 3,000hp. Metrovick also had an eye on export markets, where high ambient temperatures and high altitudes might cause the nominal output to be appreciably lower.

Drawing on experience with aircraft turbines, Metrovick's design incorporated six combustion chambers within the turbine, rather than the single combustion chamber used on No 18000. An oil of higher calorific value than the oil burned by No 18000 was required. In order to evaluate the merits of another aspect of gas-turbine design No 18100 did not have a heat-exchanger within the turbine cycle, unlike No 18000.

No 18100 had a short career, owing to its thirst for fuel. Here it roars out of Bath on 7 July 1953 with the up 'Bristolian'. *G. F. Heiron / Transport Treasury*

The turbine's running speed was 7,000rpm, and it drove three main generators at 1,600rpm through single-reduction gearing. It had two output shafts, one driving two of the main generators and the other driving the third main generator, the auxiliary generator and the exciter. Each main generator had a continuous rating of 730kW, 1,100A, 666V at 1,600rpm, and supplied a pair of traction motors, which were connected in parallel. The traction motors were suspended on the axle and from a support on the bogie frame. Each motor was rated at 490hp, 550A, 666V at 706rpm. Unlike No 18000, all three axles on each bogie were powered by a traction motor, no doubt because of the extra power produced by the turbine.

After allowing for internal losses, 2,450hp was available at the rail for traction. This equated to a balancing speed of some 85mph on level track with an 18-coach train, or 41mph up a gradient of 1 in 100 — performance little short of that of a 'Deltic'.

Construction was protracted. Although the bogies were complete and had been fitted with traction motors by July 1950, it was mid-November 1951 before the assembled and painted locomotive was ready. Delivered on 16 December 1951, it was allocated to Old Oak Common from January 1952, and during that year trials established that No 18100 could restart a 609-ton train on Hemerdon Bank; this was twice the load managed by No 18000. With a clear run from Plymouth, speed settled at from 15 to 18mph on the bank with this trailing load. Photographic evidence suggests that utilisation was primarily between Paddington and Bristol.

No 18100's active life ended in November 1953. During that month it used 700 gallons of fuel to cover a mere 214 miles — clearly an unacceptable rate of consumption. Thereafter the locomotive languished in that part of Dukinfield Carriage & Wagon Works that was rented by Metrovick but was not officially withdrawn until 1 January 1958.

A memo submitted to the BTC Works & Equipment Committee states that No 18100 showed little or no advantage in fuel costs compared with steam locomotives, while there were also issues with the complicated control gear. Metrovick attempted to simplify the control gear and to adapt the fuel system to permit the burning of cheaper grades of oil. On 12 March 1956, however, the company advised the Western Region that, given the type of turbine installed, worthwhile improvements were not possible. In the circumstances the two parties agreed to wind up the project.

A decision was taken in December 1957 to convert No 18100 into a testbed and crew-training locomotive for the 25kV AC West Coast electrification scheme between London, Birmingham, Liverpool and Manchester, which was just getting underway. In this form, renumbered first E10000 and then E2001, the locomotive enjoyed a second, equally short career, being out of use by 1962, albeit not finally withdrawn until 1968.

GT3

The Vulcan Foundry also produced a gas-turbine locomotive, this one with a mechanical drive through a 4-6-0 wheel arrangement, thus resembling a steam locomotive; it carried the number GT3. After a 12-year gestation period, trials took place during 1961. By this time, however, the locomotive was clearly out of date, matters not being helped by problems experienced during the trials.

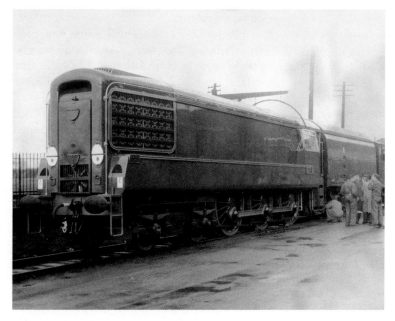

English Electric's private-venture prototype, GT3, was outdated when it finally took to the rails, owing to the lengthy construction period. Here it is seen at the company's Vulcan Foundry on 8 January 1961. *E. N. Bellass*

The APT-E — the last gas-turbine-powered train to operate in Britain – at Derby on 24 June 1972.
Brian Haresnape

The APT-E

BR's Railway Technical Centre (RTC) at Derby had developed plans for a high-speed train to the point at which the Minister of Transport announced the project in March 1967. From the start, the plan was to use gas-turbine propulsion, and by 1969 authorisation had been given to build a four-car unit, comprising two power cars and two trailers. Dubbed the APT-E (Advanced Passenger Train — Experimental), it was powered by 10 automotive gas turbines designed and built by Rolls-Royce, each delivering 300hp. Each powered bogie was fitted with two AEI 123AY traction motors.

By July 1972 the assembled unit was ready for trials, but they were delayed for a year by trade union action. Although trials did take place, and 152.3mph was achieved near Didcot on 10 August 1975, development work shifted to an all-electric version when the price of oil rose dramatically, and Leyland pulled out of gas-turbine production in 1974.

No 832

'Warship' No 832 *Onslaught* had been withdrawn in December 1972 but was appropriated by the RTC and moved to Derby in January 1973. Sister locomotive No 818 *Glory* was towed from Laira to Swindon to provide a source of spares, for it had been proposed that No 832 should be converted to gas-turbine propulsion with hydraulic transmission, but the project did not proceed.

Thus concludes our review of gas-turbine propulsion systems in railway use in Britain. This form of traction has been used elsewhere in the world, but with only limited success. The quantity of fuel oil needed to produce a meaningful amount of power for traction renders the gas turbine less efficient than the diesel engine.

Modern gas turbines have much more efficient shaft compressors, mainly because of evolving blade design and the use of more modern heat-resistant nimonic alloy steels. But they are still happier in constant-speed, constant-load regimes, as Nos 18000 and 18100 would have been; they would have performed much better if they could have worked trains at a constant 90mph over long distances, but the railway infrastructure of the day was not suitable for such a regime, and these needs seem to have been misunderstood by those behind the project. American railways afforded a better operating regime for gas-turbine traction. By the end of 1960, when the era of the gas-turbine locomotive was drawing to a close in Britain, the Union Pacific Railroad in the USA had 25 locomotives of 4,500hp and 23 double-units of 8,500hp, with more on order. Nevertheless, gas-turbine locomotives are still few in number today.

No 18100 in charge of another Western Region named train, the 'Merchant Venturer' from Paddington to Bristol, seen here raising the echoes at the east end of Twerton Tunnel on the outskirts of Bath.
G. F. Heiron / Transport Treasury

4

MECHANICAL DRIVE

Although a mechanical transmission arrangement was used quite extensively in shunting locomotives, technical factors tended to rule it out for use in main-line locomotives. In Britain, only one main-line locomotive with mechanical transmission was produced, and this was a collaboration between the LMS and a private company.

On 29 October 1947 the LMS entered into an agreement in principle with Davey Paxman & Co Ltd, the Shell Refining & Marketing Co Ltd and Lt-Col L. F. R. Fell for the construction of a 1,600hp 4-8-4 (2-D-2) diesel-mechanical locomotive that became No 10100. After Nationalisation on 1 January 1948, the newly-formed BTC had to adopt agreements such as this, and the orders for the gas-turbine locomotives described in Chapter 3. On 15 April 1948 W. J. Slim, Deputy Chairman of the Railway Executive, submitted a memorandum seeking approval to continue with the Fell collaboration, and it contains some revealing insights.

Since the date of the original agreement, the three parties concerned had formed Fell Developments Ltd. Preliminary design had reached the point at which ordering of material could begin. The special feature of the locomotive was the use of a direct mechanical drive, which was to be capable of giving higher efficiency at lower cost and weight than is the case with electric drive but eliminating gear changing, thus obviating the principal drawback in the use of mechanical drive.

The memorandum stated: 'The proposed locomotive would be similar in capacity to *the diesel-electric locomotive* already authorised for the LMR and it is proposed that when built the diesel-mechanical locomotive should be tried out *in competition with* the diesel-electric.' (Author's italics.) Thus Nos 10000 and 10001 were seen as one locomotive of two units, not two locomotives, while No 10100 was to be pitted against one 1,600hp diesel-electric unit.

The agreement between the Railway Executive and Fell Developments Ltd, which survives in the National Archives, was dated 2 July 1948 and contained the following key provisions. First, Fell Developments would provide the diesel engines, transmission and control gear at its own expense. Secondly, the LMR would design and construct the chassis portion, which comprised bogies, frames, cab and so forth. Thirdly, the locomotive would run trials for a year, and, if successful, would be acquired by the Railway Executive. If, however, the trials were deemed unsuccessful, Fell Developments would have the option of paying the LMR for the mechanical parts and take over the locomotive.

The agreement gave an estimated cost to the BTC of £25,000. H. G. Ivatt, formerly CM&EE of the LMS and now CME of the LMR, had overall charge of the design work, which was undertaken at Derby Works. Derby Order No 361 and Lot No 206 were issued. Construction on the frames started in Derby Works on 5 January 1949, and a sighting during August 1950 revealed the locomotive to be almost complete.

No 10100 embraced three fundamental principles: first, a diesel-mechanical system that aimed to eliminate the internal losses in both diesel-electric and diesel-hydraulic propulsion, in which only between 75 and 80% of engine power was actually available at the wheel rim; secondly, a multi-engine arrangement that drove through slip couplings and differential gears; and finally the use of a variable boost to the engines, so that a high boost at low speed produced high torque, with reduced boost at high speed.

Conceptually, No 10100 was a 4-8-4, with nose ends and two driving cabs. Unusually, the main propulsion engines were sited in the nose ends. They were four 12RHP Paxman diesels, each rated at 500hp at 1,500rpm, representing an increase of 100hp per engine from the original rating. Two AEC A210D six-cylinder diesels, each producing 150hp at 1,800rpm, were used to drive the Holmes-Comerville turbochargers, as well as other auxiliary functions; they were installed between the cabs. The purpose of these two engines was to enable the four main engines to apply all their output for traction purposes. Both sets of engines used the same turbochargers, so the AEC units also were subject to variable boost.

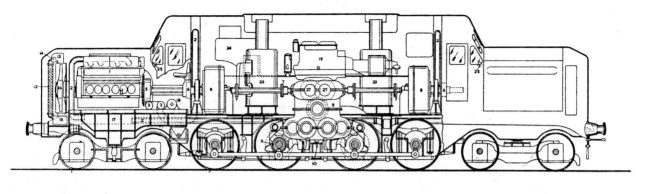

FELL DIESEL MECHANICAL LOCOMOTIVE

LAYOUT OF PROTOTYPE LOCOMOTIVE
(BRITISH RAILWAYS No. 10,100)

1	500 H.P. DAVEY PAXMAN 12 R.P.H. DIESEL ENGINES.	8	FLUID COUPLINGS, TYPE S.C.R.S. SIZE Nº 36	15	BOTTOM TANKS.	22	VACUUM EXHAUSTERS.
2	EXHAUST PIPES FOR 12 R.P.H. DIESEL ENGINES.	9	GEARBOX.	16	RADIATOR FAN.	23	TRAIN HEATING BOILERS.
3	SUPERCHARGE AIR PIPES FOR 12 R.P.H. DIESEL ENGINES.	10	REVERSING CONNECTION.	17	DIESEL OIL FUEL TANKS (CAPACITY 720 GALLONS.)	24	TRAIN HEATING BOILERS WATER TANKS (CAPY 500 GALLS.)
4	WATER CIRCULATING PUMPS.	11	QUILL DRIVING SHAFT.	18	LIFTING BRACKETS.	25	LOCOMOTIVE CONTROLS.
5	BIBBY COUPLINGS.	12	RADIATORS. (WATER ELEMENTS. OIL ELEMENTS.)	19	150 H.P. A.E.C. DIESEL AUXILIARY ENGINES.	26	CLUTCH TO RELEASE ABUTMENT OF ONE S.S.S. COUPLING
6	LAYRUB COUPLINGS.	13	WATER HEADER TANKS.	20	BEVEL GEAR BOXES FOR AUXILIARY SHAFT DRIVE.	27	SYNCHRO SELF SHIFTING COUPLINGS
7	LAYRUB COUPLINGS.	14	OIL TOP MANIFOLD.	21	HOLMES CONNERSVILLE SUPERCHARGE BLOWERS.		

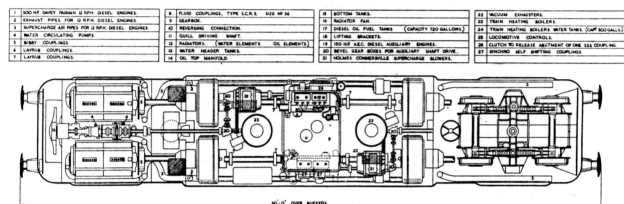

50'-0" OVER BUFFERS.

Figure 2

A radiator was positioned at the extreme end of each nose, and was driven by the AEC auxiliary engines. One radiator was coupled to one of the pairs of RPH engines and one of the AEC engines. Initially one steam generator was provided for train heating. The arrangement is illustrated schematically in the accompanying diagram.

This was certainly a novel design concept, and it offered several advantages. As with any multi-engine vehicle, failure of one engine did not cripple the locomotive. A high-speed diesel (up to 1,500rpm) could be lighter and more compact than a lower-speed diesel of comparable power. Lt-Col Fell decided to use high turbocharger boost at low speed to generate the maximum possible pulling power for starting heavy trains and climbing steep gradients. This led to a requirement for a design of engine that responded flexibly to different rates of boost and did not

experience unduly high peak cylinder pressures. Whether the Paxman RPH diesel was chosen because it offered these benefits, and whether Paxman offered its engines without payment as part of its stake within Fell Developments, or because there was no British-manufactured alternative, is open to conjecture.

In any mechanical drive, engine and road speed are correlated. In the case of No 10100 this meant that at a low road speed, the engine speed was also low, and this explains why a high boost was necessary to give high power. As the road speed rose, so did the engine speed and thus the power developed. As the boost was reduced, engine power was supposed to remain constant across the road speed range. At maximum engine speed, the boost dropped to zero. At starting, only one engine (No 3) was used, the other three cutting in progressively until all were

General Arrangement diagram of the Fell 4-8-4 diesel-mechanical locomotive, No 10100, showing the elaborate drivetrain. *BR*

powering by about 24mph. Each engine had a hydraulic coupling to permit this progression.

All four engines drove through a common mechanical transmission that used differential gears of David Brown manufacture. Three differential gears were employed, two primary differentials connected to one secondary differential. The secondary differential carried the combined power through a gear train to the driving axles, which were coupled in pairs, rendering the locomotive effectively a 4-4-4-4. Adopting this system of differentials meant that a progressively changing speed ratio was achieved without the need for an automotive type of gearbox.

A curious benefit of this ingenious design was that the maximum tractive effort was achieved at starting when, of course, only one engine was in use. Thus the failure of up to three of the RPH units would not prevent No 10100 from covering any part of its duties, albeit at a lower speed, because there would always be sufficient tractive effort to move the train.

The driver had six controls for locomotive operation: a regulator, a reverser and four small levers (referred to colloquially as 'scoops') that actuated the hydraulic couplings for each engine. With all six engines (four driving and two auxiliary) idling, the driving technique entailed first opening the regulator and then operating one of the four scoops to connect an engine into the drive train. Each scoop had a limiter at about two-thirds of full; a catch had to be released to open out to maximum. The regulator was adjusted to suit engine loading. As the speed reached predetermined levels, the other engines were brought in by moving their corresponding levers; these speeds were 6mph for the second engine, 17mph for the third and 24mph for the fourth. Top speed was quoted as 78mph. As with the other main-line prototypes of that era, the livery was black with a silver roof and lining.

The regulator was part of a pneumatic control system that was fed from the same vacuum system as the train brakes. One of the initial design failings was that this system was inadequate: as built, No 10100 could not cope

Prior to final assembly, one of the gearboxes is mounted on a pair of driving axles while inside Derby Works.
Ian Allan Library

with heavy trains, because of inadequate train brake vacuum.

No 10100's main-line debut came on 9 January 1951, but the seizure of a reversing dog clutch necessitated a return to the works four days later, with only 100 miles accumulated. On 12 February 1951, Lt-Col Fell addressed a meeting of the Institution of Mechanical Engineers in Derby. He reported that initial tests with No 10100 had proved satisfactory, and claimed the locomotive to be the first main-line diesel-mechanical machine in the world. He argued that this form of propulsion was lighter in weight per unit of horsepower, had a transmission efficiency of up to 95%, compared with 80% for a diesel-electric, and was also cheaper to build. By the date of the lecture, two weeks' worth of running had been achieved, at speeds up to 50mph. Riding was described as good, though others have disagreed. Power take-up from rest was smooth, yet the locomotive achieved rapid acceleration.

On 23 May No 10100 was on display at Marylebone for inspection by the BTC and the press, and in June it was towed to Eastbourne for exhibition at a UIC conference. Further trial trips were made during the latter half of 1951, during which time the locomotive was also exhibited at Battersea and Marylebone. While it was being serviced at Derby on 12 September, a Shell technician called to check lubrication levels but was told that the check had already been made. Regrettably a misunderstanding had arisen, because it was No 10001 that had been checked. No 10100 was taken for a trial along the Midland main line and had reached Glendon, north of Kettering, when oil starvation caused a major failure due to bearing seizure.

No 10100 was taken into British Railways stock, allocated to Derby, on 19 January 1952 for the start of the agreed one-year trial on the 21st. The inaugural run was on the 7.10am Derby–Manchester Central, the locomotive returning with the 11.15 and then working the 7.16pm to Manchester, the diagram on which it was to be deployed. Based at Derby shed, virtually all its running

No 10100 in original condition, with middle coupling rods in place. *Ian Allan Library*

was along the St Pancras and Manchester Central route. The locomotive was, however, not popular with the running staff, because of the need to find suitably-trained footplate crews, and it was convenient to cover diagrams that started and finished at Derby, hence frequent sightings on local services to Manchester over the steeply graded Peak District section, where its high power made it superior to steam.

During the first six months, during which time around 30,000 miles were accumulated, the biggest cause of unserviceability was failure of the coupling-rod bearing bushes because of the normal twisting action of the locomotive when running; this was alleviated by removing the centre rods. A far more serious incident occurred during July 1952, when a ⅞in securing screw in the secondary differential dropped into the reversing wheels while No 10100 was travelling at 50mph, causing considerable damage. In consequence, around a year was spent inside Derby Works for repairs, and the replacement gear drive had a lower ratio, to raise the starting tractive effort, but at the expense of a lower top speed of 72mph.

By the date of this failure the cost to Fell Developments was £47,500, and to the BTC £38,200. That the latter figure was £13,200 over budget was due to the addition of roller bearings on the bogies, to the provision of exhaust heaters, a second steam generator, water pick-up apparatus and auxiliary inter-cooling arrangements and to the fitting of radiators on the roof. A memorandum in the BTC's Works & Equipment Committee minutes for 10 August 1955 updated the position, the revised cost now standing at £84, 575, including outlay amounting to £46,375 over that approved already by the BTC. This arose to cover the actual cost of building the chassis and mechanical parts in British Railways workshops (£37,075) and the purchase of engines and power equipment from Fell Developments for £47,500, to which the BTC agreed at its meeting eight days later. The latter purchase had, of course, been provided for in the 1948 agreement, and the BTC's willingness to ratify this suggests that British Railways regarded the one-year

trial as a success. Moreover, the overall cost was still less than that of a comparable diesel-electric.

The September 1952 issue of *The Railway Magazine* featured a log produced by Cecil J. Allen for a working by No 10100 between Derby and Manchester Central, hauling a typical nine-coach load of 305 tons gross. Although the train was the 4.15pm from St Pancras, it is not stated whether the locomotive came on at Derby, where it was based. After the fastest start ever noted by the recorder, a signal stop caused a late arrival at Matlock.

Reflecting the steep climb into the Peak District, the 14.3 succeeding miles to Millers Dale were booked for 26 minutes, based on the use of a Class 6 steam locomotive. Demonstrating its superiority in tractive ability, No 10100 cut the schedule to 19 minutes. Observing the 45mph restriction at Rowsley, it then settled down to around 48mph on grades of between 1 in 100 and 1 in 103. This was not as good as the 50mph on the same gradient with a heavier train during some later road trials in 1954.

After Millers Dale, where the train restarted, the line steepens to 1 in 90, which is sustained to the summit at Peak Forest. No 10100 gradually reached and held 42½mph here, and this cut the booked time by 1 minute. On the run down to Didsbury, in Manchester's southern suburbs, speed was held between 64 and 72mph until a spurt saw Cheadle Heath passed at 80½mph. At this speed the coupling-rods would have been spinning furiously on the 4ft 3in driving wheels, equivalent to 120mph on a steam locomotive with 6ft 8in driving wheels!

A settled 48mph on a 1-in-100 gradient equates to 1,470edhp (equivalent drawbar horsepower), and 42½mph on a 1-in-90 to 1,400edhp. Since the external (air) resistance of the locomotive should not account for more than about 100hp at such a speed, No 10100 appears not to have been realising its 2,000hp rating. It is likely however that the driver was only opening the scoops to the limiting bar and not to full.

No 10100 was put through another series of trials in March 1954, over the Settle–

Carlisle line. Although tests were made using various combinations of the four traction diesel engines, only the results for all four engines at full power will be given here. The trials found that the four RPH diesels were developing up to 2,230hp. The maximum drawbar horsepower was 1,900 at 44mph, which is high for a locomotive with a nominal brake horsepower of 2,000. The starting tractive effort was 29,400lb. At speeds between 30mph and 65mph, the drawbar tractive effort was superior both to the prototype diesel-electric No 10203, of similar installed power, and to a Class 7 'Britannia' Pacific steam locomotive.

Specific fuel consumption (in pounds per drawbar horsepower hour) for all six engines was very similar to the test results for the Southern Region diesel of 1,750hp, rising from 0.53 at 30mph to 0.59 at 60mph, as against 0.51 and 0.62 at these speeds for the diesel-electric. Hauling the maximum timetabled load for a '6P' steam locomotive

of 389 tons between Appleby and Ais Gill, the locomotive cut the schedule of 30 minutes to 25½min, while the speed of 50mph on the 1-in-100 gradient between these points was superior to what No 10203 could achieve.

These trials demonstrated that No 10100 had a very efficient transmission, but only over a limited speed range. Above 65mph the drawbar tractive effort fell steeply from about 10,000lb to zero at 72mph, making it unsuitable for high-speed passenger duties.

After the trials Lt-Col Fell wrote in the *Railway Gazette* that, although No 10100 was referred to as a 2,000hp unit, this was rather misleading. The maximum power taken from each of the Paxman engines was 570hp, and from each of the AEC engines 150hp. Absolute maximum power was, however, not available from all the main engines together at any speed, though this was to be the case on any future units.

The April 1956 report produced by the LMR on its main-line diesels, which was

No 10100 at Eastbourne, one of three locations (the others being Battersea and Marylebone) at which it was exhibited in 1951.
Rail Photoprints

referred to in Chapter 2, also covered No 10100. Between 7 May 1955 and 28 January 1956, the locomotive covered 22,168 miles running between St Pancras and Manchester, but its availability was a lamentable 22.5%. Nevertheless, No 10100 suffered from markedly fewer design and manufacturing problems than its diesel-electric cousins, while there were no reported issues attributable to inadequate or incorrect maintenance or operation.

After having been out of traffic for over a year from August 1956, No 10100's end came on 16 October 1958, when its steam generator caught fire at Manchester Central. Although the damage could have been repaired cheaply, the locomotive was withdrawn on 22 November 1958. Management had lost interest in it, and the running staff often needed to be persuaded to use it; in short, its time was up. Although

Lt-Col Fell had plans for improved designs, one of which incorporated hydraulic transmission in the drive train, they never materialised.

No 10100 ran for only around 80,000 miles, which was a disappointing total, not helped by the major failures it suffered, but the lower boost pressure at higher speeds appears to have meant that the RPH engines caused less trouble than the unit installed in No 10800. It must not be overlooked that, all told, there were 60 cylinders to maintain and potentially cause trouble. In conclusion, the locomotive achieved what it was designed to do. But by the time this was established, the world had moved on. If the long periods out of traffic, due to unfortunate accidents, had been avoided, No 10100's worth might have been more greatly appreciated and taken forward. It proved to be the sole line-service diesel-mechanical machine to run in Britain.

Now minus the middle coupling rods, No 10100 powers through Didsbury, in the southern suburbs of Manchester, with a train from Manchester Central to St Pancras on 12 January 1954.
N. Dyckhoff

5

TRANSMISSION WARS

Before proceeding to review the momentous events that revolutionised the British railway-motive-power scene, beginning in the mid-1950s, it is important to appreciate something of the technical background to the decisions taken. What follows therefore sets out the arguments for and against diesel-electric and diesel-hydraulic transmissions, as expressed during the second half of the 1950s and first half of the 1960s; these are not the author's views but those of contemporary writers. After that date, transmission choices for rail applications had largely polarised between diesel-electric for line-service diesel locomotives and (increasingly) hydraulic drive for self-propelled railcars, with shunting locomotives continuing to show no strong inclination in either direction.

Part of the reason was technical progress in the field of electronics, notably in AC power conversion and its application to rail traction drives, which put the balance of advantage in terms of high tractive effort firmly with electric drive for locomotives. These developments will be outlined later. Of course, it is not only a case of electric versus hydraulic but also a contrast between two very different forms of hydraulic drive, the multi-stage converter versus the single converter with mechanical gearbox. Or perhaps just hydrodynamic and hydromechanical.

Some key issues

Continuous rating

An important factor in reliable locomotive operation is the speed at which full power can be sustained indefinitely — the continuous rating. With DC power generators and traction motors fitted to mixed-traffic diesel-electrics, the continuous rating was invariably

Below: The high-revving 16-cylinder Bristol-Siddeley Maybach MD870 engine, with a UIC rating of 2,000hp at 1,500rpm, as supplied for use in the 'Hymek' Type 3 diesel-hydraulics. *Bristol Siddeley*

Left: Presenting a contrast in sizes, here is the slow-speed 16-cylinder English Electric SVT engine, which evolved over the years from 1,600hp at 750rpm in Nos 10000 and 10001 through to a UIC rating of 3,520hp at 900rpm in Mk III form. Here a Class 50 16CSVT Mk II and generator undergo overhaul at Doncaster Works during 1982. *Author's collection*

achieved at a higher engine speed than with a comparable diesel-hydraulic with the same maximum speed and installed power. The combination of trailing load and ruling gradient are key elements in determining the ability of a locomotive to perform reliably, because if the result is a sustained speed below the continuous rating, the transmission will overheat and ultimately fail. Operators need to have a traction unit that can haul the required load over the designated route without overheating.

Adhesion weight

The adhesion weight of a locomotive is the weight on its powered axles; weight on unpowered axles does not contribute towards adhesion. Adhesion is needed to get a train started and then accelerate it to line speed. Overall adhesion weight is therefore important, but it needs to be balanced against the wish for a locomotive to be no heavier than it needs to be for the work envisaged. Maximum tractive effort is often expressed as a percentage of total adhesion weight. During the period in question the value established by dynamometer-car trials was about 27½% for both diesel-electrics and diesel-hydraulics. For train-planning purposes, to determine maximum train loads the Western Region assumed a maximum adhesion factor of 24% for locomotives with sanding gear and 22% for those without.

Transmission efficiency

Transmission efficiency is a product of the design, and is the amount of power delivered to the wheels expressed as a percentage of the gross (bhp) output of all the installed diesel engines; the higher the percentage, the more efficient the transmission. Losses arise from the creation of unwanted heat within the drive train (electric motors or torque-converter, as examples) and the effect of mechanical friction. Efficiency is not a constant value, but generally varies by a few points across the speed range. Most commentators at the time accepted that generally there was no *significant* advantage between electric and hydraulic drive (in its different forms), and efficiency values of a

couple of percentage points either side of 80% were normal. Transmission design governed its efficiency, so not all diesel-electrics were equally efficient.

Transmission design

Designers of transmissions have to take into consideration the speed range over which a locomotive will be required to operate, and to produce a transmission that will give a performance characteristic that best suits the applications envisaged. This is easiest for a specialist locomotive, such as one intended purely for low- or high-speed service; it is most difficult for a mixed-traffic machine, in which there are inevitably compromises between high starting efforts, low continuous rating speeds and an ability to haul trains at high speed. Over the 80 years of the application of hydraulic drive in rail vehicles, the balance of advantage has swung both ways at different times, though it has probably favoured the diesel-electric drive for the most part.

Transmission cooling

Cooling the transmission components helps to lower the continuous rating. It is easier to dissipate heat in hydraulic transmission systems than in electrical machines.

Maintenance

The locomotive needs maintenance and repair, electrical and hydraulic equipment needing quite different regimes. Quick-running engines, which have inevitably (but not exclusively) been associated with hydraulic transmission, are much lighter than slow-speed diesels of comparable power. The lifting facilities needed to remove a quick-running engine are less substantial than are needed to lift a slow-speed engine of comparable power.

Locomotive weight

A lightweight locomotive may be no better than an overweight one, depending on the operating environment, so light weight is not always good. Lightweight locomotives are much less suitable for handling unbraked freights than heavier machines.

Above: A low overall weight meant a low locomotive brake force for handling unfitted freights. It is likely that this train had a fitted head to augment the braking of 'Hymek' No D7053.
Ian Allan Library

Left: With unbraked trains, locomotive brake force is important. It was the low brake force of the Western Region's 'D7000' class that let the BR Standard Type 3 gain a foothold in the region for hauling South Wales mineral traffic. Seen near Pontycymmer, No 37 220 heads a loaded coal train, still unbraked on 25 March 1976. *G. T. Heavyside*

Above: Although low power-to-weight ratios are less important for unbraked freight operation, the converse is true for high-speed passenger services. When compared to contemporary WR-built Type 4s, the English Electric No D200s were, effectively a coach-and-a-half inferior by virtue of their 133-ton bulk. On 8 June 1960 No D223 races the traffic on a nearly empty M1 with an up service from Liverpool Lime Street. *Derek Cross*

Transmission types — electric

The principles of diesel-electric transmission in DC form are generally fairly well known. A diesel engine output shaft turns the armature shaft of a main generator, which generates current in the armature. The electricity is delivered by cables to the traction motors that turn the axles. Traditionally, the traction motors were axle-hung, nose-suspended for simplicity, and this arrangement offers the highest transmission efficiency. Of course, there are disadvantages: axle-hung, nose-suspended motors punish the track, and also cause transfer in axle loading at starting and during periods of high tractive effort. Such a transfer in axle loading has an impact on adhesion weight, which is reduced on some axles and makes them more prone to slip. Modern high-power locomotive design has moved away from this arrangement for traction motor suspension in favour of mounting the motors on the bogies or within the locomotive body, with cardan shafts transmitting the power to the axles. In Britain the Class 91s were the first electric locomotives to have such an arrangement.

The inherent characteristics of the series-wound DC motor make it readily adaptable to traction duties, and the motor armature shaft may be geared directly to the road wheels. Maximum torque is available at stall, and depends to some extent on the current capacity of the motor. Torque is dependent on motor current — the higher the current, the higher the torque — while torque declines as speed rises. Increasing the armature rotation speed creates an opposing force — the back electromotive force (back EMF) — which can be compensated for by increasing the voltage at which the motor is supplied. Eventually the back EMF reaches the point at which the maximum supply voltage is reached — the 'unloading point' of the main generator. To provide a broad speed range, the field in the motor windings is weakened to reduce the back EMF by the use of electrical resistances (field weakening). The number of stages of field weakening depends on the design of the electrical machines, and progressive stages of weakening are used as speed rises. Operation of the DC traction motors at high speeds compounds the problem of mechanical vibration through unsprung mounting with high voltage, leading to poor commutation and increased risk of flashover, potentially causing severe damage; thus, historically, designers were faced with a compromise between providing a wide speed range for the locomotive and the risk that extending the range of operation of the motor by field weakening beyond a certain point would bring problems of motor reliability. More modern DC traction drives, such as those in the HST, avoid the use of field weakening.

Transmission types — hydraulic

The work of Hermann Föttinger during the first two decades of the 20th century was defining for rail traction. It began in northern Germany in 1905 while he was designing a transmission system suitable for transmitting the output of marine steam turbines to the propeller shafts. Two patents were taken out that year — one for a hydraulic torque-converter, the other for a fluid coupling.

Concentrating on the torque-converter for German Navy application, the potential of the fluid coupling went unrecognised for many years, but it was to prove a key component not only in hydraulic but also in mechanical transmissions. It was, however, Harold Sinclair who, from 1926, took up the idea of the fluid coupling, and eventually introduced it into rail use around 1930. Meanwhile, the use of the torque-converters in the marine application for which they had been devised faded away within a few years, by reason of other technical advances.

In the mid-1920s Föttinger was approached by several German engineering companies seeking to exploiting his patents. Although Voith came to an agreement with Föttinger in 1929 the first rail application did not come until 1933, when torque-converter drive was used in railcars for Österreichische Bundesbahnen (Austrian State Railways), as noted in Chapter 1.

From 1928 Alfred Lysholm began to develop the Föttinger torque-converter; his main contribution was in the design of the turbine blades, which improved the efficiency of the converter. Lysholm also originated the three-stage converter and the use of direct drive for the upper end of the road speed range. Of course, direct drive (as evidenced by No 10100) is the most efficient form of transmission. Lysholm can therefore be credited with devising the first hydro-mechanical transmission. Multiple-stage turbine blading enabled the torque-speed characteristic to become automatically variable within a wide range of high efficiency.

In Britain, Leyland Motors took forward the Lysholm system with the addition of direct drive. It was this type of transmission that was used in the LMS railcar of 1938. It was developed further by the Twin Disc Clutch Co of the USA, and this design of hydraulic drive will, like Voith's developments, be referred to in the designs of the 1950s and later.

How a torque-converter works

A torque-converter does not use high oil pressure to deliver power; rather it operates using principles of fluid dynamics. It consists of three parts: (*a*) an impeller (pump), driven directly by the input shaft (*i.e.* the output shaft from the diesel engine); (*b*) a turbine wheel, or driven member, which is coupled to the torque-converter output shaft; and (*c*) a set of reaction or guide vanes, which are fixed within the converter casing. The volume

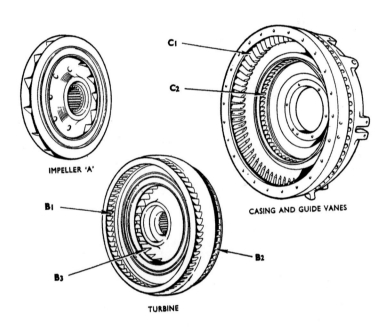

The three elements of a Rolls-Royce hydrodynamic torque-converter. 'A' is the impeller, which is driven by the engine; it has one ring of blades, which pump the fluid (invariably oil) with which the converter is filled. 'B' is the turbine, made up of three rings of blades, B1, B2 and B3, which is connected to the output, or driven, shaft. The reaction member on the housing has two rings of guide vanes, C1 and C2, attached to the stationary casing. When the input shaft is driven, the impeller blades force the fluid outwards, striking the first ring of turbine blades, B1. The fluid, having changed direction to give initial torque to the turbine, is then redirected by the first set of guide vanes, C1, to impinge on the second set of turbine blades, B2, adding more torque to the turbine. Again the fluid is redirected, this time by the second ring of guide vanes. C2, to the turbine blades, B3. In operating conditions, when the output speed is approaching its maximum, the fluid passes quickly around the circuit, striking each blade at only a small angle to the normal. As the load on the output shaft increases, the turbine slows down, the striking angle is increased, and the output torque rises. *Ian Allan Library*

1. **Input**
2. **Torque Converter**
3. **Hydrodynamic Coupling**
4. **Filler Pump**
5. **Reversing Mechanism**
6. **Output**

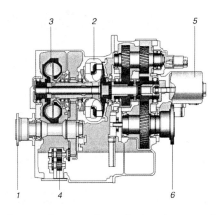

Above: Vertical section through a torque-converter, in this case the Voith T211rzz, used in 'Sprinter', 'Networker Turbo' and 'Turbostar' DMUs. *Voith*

Below: The Voith L630rV torque-converter, as fitted in the 'D1000' ('Western') class. *Voith*

inside is taken up by oil. As the impeller rotates, the converter fluid is accelerated outwards, and its energy becomes available at the converter output shaft via the turbine wheel. To complete the circuit the fluid is deflected for re-entry into the impeller by the guide vanes. Since the system overall is stable, the reaction torque at the guide vanes must provide the torque difference between the input and output shafts.

The output torque is at its maximum when the turbine wheel, or output shaft, is stalled. As the train is accelerated, the converter's output torque falls off smoothly and automatically. In order to cover a wide speed range, one converter operating on a fixed output gear ratio is insufficient. Two methods have been devised to overcome this.

The first solution, which is more in keeping with a hydraulic transmission, is to use the characteristics of three converters, one for starting and two (successively) for 'running'; this is usually referred to as a hydrodynamic system. The torque multiplications obtained are dependent on the design of the impeller and turbine blading and this, in turn, influences the efficiency obtainable. The starting converter is designed to provide high torque multiplication (high tractive effort). The second and third converters display broader efficiency curves and flatter torque curves. Depending on the application, one or another combination of torque-converters and fluid couplings, or a series of torque-converters without fluid couplings, may be used. Where more than one hydraulic circuit is used, the automatic changeover between circuits is achieved by emptying and filling the respective circuits. Emptying and filling each converter, to bring it into or take it out of use, is controlled by the transmission governor, a device that reacts to rail and engine speed. Voith transmissions are of this type.

The second method of obtaining an acceptable speed range is to employ a single converter and a multi-speed mechanical gearbox, an arrangement that is often termed a hydromechanical drive. A typical example is the Maybach Mekydro transmission, which employs a single converter and a four-speed mechanical gearbox. It is claimed that it has the advantage over the multiple-converter arrangement (*e.g.* Voith) in that it is cheaper and simpler for the same number of transmission ratios, and does not necessitate constantly emptying and filling converters, to the detriment of the oil by aeration. All the elements of the transmission, including the automatic control mechanism, are housed in a single enclosed oil-tight casing of cast iron. Proponents of the hydrodynamic system counter by arguing that the emptying and filling of converter circuits gives interruption-free torque, whereas the gear changes within the hydromechanical drive cause a transitory break in tractive effort, which can cause coupling snatch. The oil sump for a hydrodynamic system is much larger than that of a fully enclosed hydromechanical torque-converter, and so oil degradation due to aeration is not a real problem.

Looking now in some detail at the working of a hydromechanical system – in this case the Mekydro system – the impeller of the torque-converter, which is filled with oil, is driven by the engine through a 2:1 step-up gear and a hollow shaft. The step-up gear enables the dimensions of the converter to be kept within reasonable limits, the diameter over the converter casing being only about 22in.

The turbine member has two rows of blades — one for the normal drive, the other to produce a weak reverse torque during gear-changing operations. The main row of turbine blades is in alignment with the impeller blades when the member is in position, the other row coming into operation when the other member is pushed over to one side. The longitudinal movement of the turbine member is controlled by a plunger at its centre that is fed with oil under pressure, and its rotational movement is transmitted to the mechanical gearbox by through splines on the output shaft, which revolves inside the hollow shaft of the impeller.

The gear train required is selected from three pairs of wheels, each pair being in constant mesh, by causing the claw clutches between those wheels to dispose themselves in any one of four possible combinations of positions.

The two wheels that are in constant mesh with the driver wheels, together with the two other claw clutches, constitute the reversing mechanism, the direction of rotation of wheels being determined by the positioning of these two clutches. Two output flanges transmit the power through cardan shafts and bevel-wheel final drives to the axles of the bogie.

A gear-type pump, driven from the input gear, supplies oil to the control mechanism, keeps the converter circuit pressure-filled and provides lubrication for the gears and bearings of the transmission.

The control mechanism, which works by oil pressure, initiates gear changes fully automatically and in such a way that the relationship between the converter impeller and turbine speeds is maintained within the limits needed to ensure efficient operation over nearly the whole speed range of the locomotive. The stages of a gear change proceed as follows. The two parts of the governor are driven by the primary and secondary sides of the torque-converter through appropriate gearing. When the ratio of the speeds of these two sides (*i.e.* the ratio between engine speed and road speed in any given gear) falls outside a predetermined value, the governor actuates a gear selector valve, which admits oil to the gear selector, moving it by one notch one way or the other depending on whether the gear is to be changed up or down. Thereafter, the gear selector supplies oil to the gear-change cylinders, which operate the clutch selector forks. The force available for moving the clutches is not, however, sufficient to disengage them while the transmission is under load, and the necessary unloading is effected by the oil pressure to the cylinder,

Maybach Mekydro K184 torque-converter, as fitted in the 'Hymeks'. *Maybach*

also operating the torque-converter engagement valve simultaneously through the converter locking valve, causing the converter turbine to take up the disengaged position as previously explained. The clutches can now be parted by the force of the operating mechanism, and consequently the selector fork in question moves to effect the parting, at the same time causing the halves of the opposite clutch to approach each other. For reasons that will be explained later these halves cannot engage until their speeds are synchronised. Accordingly, as an upward or downward gear change is being made the forward or backward blading of the turbine is now engaged for a short time by a control impulse produced by the piston of the cylinder in its intermediate position. By this means the driving half of the clutch is accelerated or decelerated until its speed is equal to that of the other half. The clutch then engages, so allowing the selector fork to complete its movement. The pistons also reach their full travel, and in this position they cause the converter turbine to take up its working position. The gear-change procedure, which takes only a very short time, is then complete.

The faces of the teeth on both the driving and the driven half are slightly inclined, so that if the driving half is moving faster than the other half, the two parts continually push each other away until the speeds are synchronised. The axial movements and therefore the longitudinal forces called into play by this action are minimised by the use of a baulk ring.

The Mekydro system was developed by Maybach in 1938. In both the full hydraulic and the hydromechanical variants power is transmitted to the axles by cardan shafts. Until the late 1950s manufacturers of hydraulic transmission did not produce equipment with an input capacity of more than 1,000hp, and it was this, rather than engine capacity, that limited the power of a locomotive.

Transmission types — mechanical

Mechanical drive offers high efficiencies, but in a 'change-speed' gear drive there is the issue of reduced engine speed after changing up a gear, and the drop in tractive effort when this takes place. In any one-gear step, full engine power is available at high engine speed and not at the low engine speed, just after a change-up to a higher range; hence gear-step mechanical transmissions have always been confined to applications of low power (shunters) or high power per ton (railcars). On No 10100 this limitation was overcome by the use of fluid couplings and variable boost in the engines.

Pros and cons

By virtue of its design, the torque-converter has no mechanical connection between the revolving pump impellers and the turbine runners or the stationary reaction vanes, so there is practically no wear, and no increase in the clearances between the stationary and the moving parts. Because the fluid circuit is enclosed there is no prospect of the ingress of foreign material, such as water or brake dust. By contrast, traction motors require a flow of air for cooling and so cannot be completely enclosed or free from the ingress of foreign material.

Hydraulic transmission is generally simpler to maintain, and does not require the specialist repair facility that is needed to deal with the failure of electrical machines. Electrical machines are also more susceptible to moisture in the machine windings. A torque-converter, having no brushgear to be maintained, essentially needs just to be topped up with oil from time to time. The control scheme for a diesel-hydraulic is less complex, and so more reliable, than for a diesel-electric.

The traditional arrangement of an axle-hung traction motor merely entailed running a power cable from the generator. By contrast, a hydraulic drive needed the provision of a series of cardan shafts to transmit the power from the torque-converter or gearbox to the axles.

Comparing the traction characteristics of diesel-electric and diesel-hydraulic transmission during the 1950s and 1960s, the diesel-hydraulic had an inherent ability of delivering high starting tractive effort up to adhesion weight, yet was also capable of 90mph; and since both the speed at which full engine output could be absorbed by the transmission and the speed at which this maximum output could be held continuously were generally lower, diesel-hydraulics had the edge in hauling heavy loads up a gradient at low speed. Part of the reason for this lay in the ability of the transmission oil to dissipate the resultant heat more effectively than was the case in most locomotives with traction motors, in which heat dissipation from the copper windings was more difficult.

For the same reasons, a hydraulic drive could sustain a high transitory tractive effort for longer than could a drive with traction motors, which could be damaged if pushed for too long beyond their sustainable limit. This was important when determining the 'break-away' tractive effort, that is, the effort needed to get a train started, when it might take time for the brakes to release fully.

Maximum starting tractive effort dictates maximum train weight, and is influenced by the installed power of the locomotive, the transmission type and the factor of adhesion attainable by the locomotive in the prevailing conditions. With hydraulic drive, the axles of each bogie are connected by cardan shafts, which is generally not the case with electric drive; hence there was no possibility of a single axle slipping, which was frequently the case with an axle-hung traction motor drive. In fact, once an axle starts to slip, this can induce load-shedding from other axles.

In the 1950s hydraulic drive gave a smooth but rapid build-up of power, whereas in those pre-electronics days, electric drive tended to be more abrupt in its application. It is claimed that the inherent shape of the tractive effort/speed curve of the hydraulic transmission falls away sharply as speed rises, and is thus naturally responsive to wheelslip. By contrast, there is nothing in the tractive-effort/speed curve of a traditionally wound traction motor that would cause the power to be reduced if slipping occurred.

High tractive effort can cause considerable alteration in axle loadings between the bogies. This is caused by difference in height between the points of power application in the bogies and at the drawbar. It is often called 'sitting back', because the locomotive lifts slightly on its leading bogie. With downward pressure on the trailing bogie nearest the drawbar; the effect is to make the axles on the leading bogie more prone to slip because of the lower weight on them. Having all the axles on a bogie connected by cardan shafts reduces the risk of such slipping, which is another advantage over the nose-suspended traction motor.

A diesel-hydraulic transmission could provide a high tractive effort of 24 to 27% adhesion (*i.e.* percentage of total adhesion weight) at 15% of the maximum permitted speed, even when that was up to 90mph. This was not possible with diesel-electric transmission until the 1970s. Hydraulic transmission is lighter than electric transmission, but this can be a disadvantage if it results in an adhesion weight that is too low for the required duties.

The dead weight of the locomotive is not, of course, the whole story when applying the laws of motion to trains, since, in addition to providing linear acceleration, some parts of the locomotive require rotational acceleration as well. For the diesel-electric, the rotating parts comprise the wheels and axles, the traction motor armatures, gears, etc, while for the hydraulic they includes all cardan shafts, couplings and gears and the converter components.

Once the inertia of these rotating parts has been evaluated, their equivalent mass (the mass that would represent the rotating parts in linear motion) can be arrived at. One commentator (in a paper by P. J. S. Fordham of Brush Electrical Engineering Ltd to the Institution of Locomotive Engineers in 1963) gave the value of this equivalent mass as 14% of locomotive weight for a diesel-hydraulic and 4-5% for a diesel-electric. Irrespective of whether the value for the diesel-hydraulic is too high (because it would imply more than 15 tons of rotating parts in the drive train), this suggests that some of the weight advantage of the diesel-hydraulic is lost during acceleration, because power is required to accelerate this additional equivalent mass. This extra equivalent mass also acts like a flywheel in opposing deceleration during braking.

6

GERMAN INFLUENCE

J. M. Voith GmbH & Co KG

Johann Matthäus Voith took over a locksmith's shop from his father in 1825. He had a broader interest in engineering matters, and during the 1840s he began to develop paper-making machinery, of which water flows are an integral part; he later began to take an interest in fluid power. Voith signed over his business to his son in 1867, and this is the year in which the present business is regarded as having been established.

Difficult trading conditions during World War 1 led Voith to diversify into power-transmission systems. The year 1922 saw the first production of geared transmissions. With the employment of fluid flows, speed and torque were transmitted efficiently and virtually without wear. Collaboration with Professor Föttinger, the inventor and patent-holder of the hydrodynamic torque-converter and hydrodynamic coupling (see Chapter 5), began in 1929 and led to the production of a 38,000hp hydrodynamic coupling, which was used in pump-storage power plants. Design of equipment for rail and road applications began in 1930.

When the North British Locomotive Co went into liquidation on 19 April 1962 contracts for the supply of complete locomotives and transmissions to British Railways remained unfulfilled. Voith set up a manufacturing subsidiary in part of NBL's Queen's Park Works in Glasgow to complete these orders and deal with warranty and servicing work.

Voith remains a global engineering player. During the opening decade of the 21st century its turbines were installed in the famous Three Gorges Dam project on China's Yangtze River, one of the largest dams in the world. The company is one of the three largest manufacturers of paper-making machinery globally, and Voith Turbo remains a major player in transmission design and manufacture, notably for rail applications.

German railway practice

When considering the alternatives for rail traction drive, the significance of German practice cannot be overlooked, because it had such a bearing on events in Britain during the main period of dieselisation and beyond. Whereas British Railways ended up with a multiplicity of diesel locomotive designs, DB had just one in each of the power categories, and each of them had an equivalent in Britain. A brief examination of German development and practice will therefore serve to put the British experience in context.

In 1948 Deutsche Bundesbahn (German Federal Railways, reconstituted from the West German part of the prewar Reichsbahn) decided to opt for hydraulic transmission for main-line traction, for both railcars and locomotives. The decision was based on experience before World War 2 with various forms of drive, against the background of an overriding need for economy in operation. Factors influencing the decision were the low weight of hydraulic drive and its small space requirement, and because the first cost was markedly lower than that of a diesel-electric equivalent. Factors contributing to the reliability of the system were robustness of design, simplicity of control and minimal maintenance. In operation, the inherent design characteristics offered efficient wheelslip protection. Additionally, DB felt that hydraulic drive design had progressed, whereas electrical machine design had not. A major issue in progressing dieselisation, regardless of the type of transmission, was that fuel oil cost six times as much as coal.

The 'V80s' and 'V100s'

Starting in 1951, DB introduced a class of, initially, 10 locomotives of between 800 and 1,000hp, which had a single cab and were mounted on two B-B bogies. Conceptually, these drew on developments in both engine and hydraulic transmission technology during the previous decade, and the layout was configured so that engines and transmissions of different manufacture could be used interchangeably.

The three engines chosen were the Maybach MD650, the MAN L12V17.5/22B and the Daimler-Benz MB.820AB, rated respectively at 1,000hp at 1,500rpm, 800hp at 1,400rpm and 800hp at 1,400rpm. As an aside, the 12-cylinder MD650 was the same overall size as the Paxman 12-cylinder RPH engine fitted into LMR prototype No 10100, yet the Daimler-Benz was rated at twice the output of the other.

Maybach had developed its Mekydro system, first applied in a 600hp power van built in 1938. The K.104 fitted in the V80s had a permanently filled torque-converter and a four-speed mechanical drive. Meanwhile, Voith had been working to take account of the impact of the addition of turbocharging to a diesel engine. This made it necessary to have a three-stage torque-converter to achieve sufficient starting tractive effort, and brought forth the Voith T36r model, first introduced in May 1951 in two railcars. In late 1953 the T36r was replaced by the L306r, which was used in the 'V80' locomotives without a fluid coupling.

The final drive had two gear ratios, which offered top speeds of 31 and 62mph. The overall weight varied between 60 and 61 tons, depending on the equipment installed; a bogie design without a centre pivot was used. The V80s provided DB with valuable experience, not least in the design and choice of materials for cardan shafts, which presented a source of problems. Eventually the basic design was multiplied to become the standard secondary-line traction unit, with later builds having more powerful charge-cooled engines.

The 'V200s'

The initial success of the 'V80s' led DB to consider a 2,000hp design suitable for lightweight, fast passenger and parcels trains that would cover long distances. A combination of (for the time) modern engines, transmissions and mechanical parts made the proposal viable because the resultant locomotive would be lightweight, whereas 'traditional' diesel-electric locomotives of the period would have been heavy, and therefore uneconomic on light trains. The target was to produce a traction unit of 80 tons capable of achieving a maximum tractive effort of up to 30% of adhesion weight.

Initially five prototypes were ordered in 1952 and deliveries began during 1953. The same engines and transmissions as were fitted in the 'V80s' were to be used in the new machines, and the mechanical design had to cater for this interchangeability. In the event, the MAN engine was never used in a 'V200', for the five prototypes all had the Mekydro K104 transmission. For the 'V200s', the Voith L306r torque-converter was modified by locating the main output shaft low down on the unit; the modified version was first fitted in three 'V200s' during April 1955.

Krauss Maffei undertook the construction, and monocoque (stressed-skin) construction techniques were employed. This approach had been developed for aircraft construction, and used the body as part of the support structure rather than relying purely on a strength underframe to carry all the weight of everything above solebar height. A double-cab arrangement was specified, and the 'V80' bogie was modified to take account of a longer, heavier locomotive travelling at up to 140km/h (87mph); it had a 37in wheel diameter. The overall weight was between 72 and 76 tons. The starting tractive effort was calculated as 56,800lb, and the continuous tractive effort was 44,800lb at 11.8mph. The first two created quite a stir when they were exhibited at Munich in 1953, by virtue of the combination of their high power and their light weight. All five were built by early 1954, and went into commercial service from April. One of the duties involved hauling a train of 450 tons over a route with a ruling gradient of 1 in 50 and sharp curvature.

Trials during 1954 established a maximum tractive effort of 63,000lb on a dry, sanded rail, while restarting a 1050-ton train on a 1-in-100 gradient, which produced a drawbar effort of 54,500lb before slipping. A 475-ton train was restarted and hauled successfully for 3.3 miles at a gradient of between 1 in 50 and 1 in 49. The continuous-rating speed was established as 12mph, and the drawbar pull at 87mph was 4,500lb. The thermal efficiency was estimated to be roughly five times that of the steam type being displaced, though prevailing oil and coal prices wiped out this efficiency gain.

Early results were very good, the design having built on experience with the 'V80s', notably in cardan shaft design. By the late 1950s re-diagramming saw the class on inter-zonal services, with loads up to 600 tons and extensive use of full power in the mid- and high-speed ranges. One issue with the Voith L306r was that it had a small oil sump and numerous gears, which were already highly stressed. The small oil sump proved inadequate to cope with the constant full loading, the result being excessive oil temperatures and premature oil degradation. This led to premature wear on gear teeth, increasing 'play' in the gear assemblies, which in turn caused loosening of rivets in the turbines and consequential damage. The solution to the problem was to increase the oil throughput, and between 1961 and 1962 the L306rB transmission was substituted in the 'V200s', which incorporated several other modifications, including revisions to the turbine blades and gears.

Another transmission issue emerged shortly afterwards, when certain pairs of gear wheels showed signs of wear, coupled with high-frequency vibration. It was found that the problem related to running at full load for long periods in the second hydraulic stage; during this period the gears were being supplied with insufficient oil. As a result of the counter-pressure caused by the high speed of the converter pump wheel and turbine runner, against the filling pressure of the feed pump that was used for filling this circuit, the oil throughput became insufficient for effective lubrication. Converting the system from external to internal filling solved the problem.

By 1962 a total of 86 'V200s' were achieving 90% availability and an average across the fleet of 148,000 miles per locomotive per year. They were deployed mainly on express passenger diagrams, on which the train weight could vary from 250 to 650 tons, while on the Black Forest route, with a ruling gradient of 1 in 50 and sharp curves, freight trains of 605 tons were handled. Reliability on the DB definition (no failure requiring assistance) improved from 65,000 miles in 1957 to 196,000 miles in 1960.

DB 'V200' No V200.022 heads a southbound express on the Hamburg–Osnabrück line near Vehrte on 31 May 1968.
J. L. McIvor

The 'V60s'

On the basis of the early experience with the 'V80s', in 1954 DB was sufficiently confident to order more than 250 locomotives of a new design for station- and yard-pilot work. An 0-6-0 wheel arrangement was chosen, and the powertrain comprised (initially) a Maybach GTO6 of 650hp at 1,400rpm, coupled to a Voith L37zUb hydraulic transmission. The overall weight was around 50 tons, and the top speed was 37mph. Ultimately 942 of the class were built.

ML3000

During 1957 Krauss-Maffei built a C-C version of the 'V200' design, with two Maybach MD650 engines, each of 1,100hp, and two sets of Mekydro hydraulic transmission, the locomotive having an overall weight of 96 tons. The Semmering route in Austria was selected for trials, which were on service trains of up to 600 tons, all handled unassisted despite a ruling gradient of 1 in 40. Drawbar pulls up to 74,000lb were achieved, although the calculated maximum was 66,000lb.

In 1958 Krauss Maffei re-equipped the locomotive with two Maybach MD655 engines, each developing 1,500hp at 1,500rpm, which were intercooled versions of the earlier MD650s. During the summer of that year Maybach had unveiled the new Mekydro K184 transmission, which could accept an input of up to 1,800hp and was therefore capable of absorbing the higher output from an MD655. The 'V200' six-notch power controller was replaced by one with 15 positions. The gross weight now became 103 tons, and the number ML3000 was ascribed. Further trials on service trains established a balancing speed of 19.3mph on a gradient of between 1 in 53 and 1 in 50 with a 750-ton train. While the locomotive was at rest and with the train brakes on, full power was applied gradually, and a pull of 84,000lb was achieved, yet even after three minutes the transmission oil was still at normal temperature. Restarting a 600-ton train on a 1-in-42 required only 1,920hp and a tractive effort of 59,000lb, while full engine output was available by 7½mph.

Krauss-Maffei prototype ML2200, which became ML3000 in 1958 after being fitted with two MD655 engines. *Krauss-Maffei AG*

The 'V160s'

By the end of the 1950s the application of charge-air cooling meant that a 2,000hp locomotive could be built with only one engine, whereas the 'V200s' had needed two. One powertrain halved the maintenance costs of two, which delivered the same power combined, and it could be accommodated in a 75-ton B-B design. By October 1958 Voith had developed a new transmission, the L218rS, which was capable of an input of 1,800hp, and it was used in the first six 'V160s', coupled to a 16-cylinder Maybach MD870/1B diesel of 1,900hp at 1,500rpm. Intended for general use, the transmission was arranged to enable either a 50mph top speed for freight duties or 75mph for passenger and parcels work. No 160.001 entered traffic during May 1960, and, with

Right: The 'German Hymek', No V160.001, with MD 870 engine but Voith L218 transmission, which appeared in the summer of 1960. *Voith*

Right: Henschel prototype No V320.001, which when built in 1962 took from the English Electric 'Deltics' the mantle of the world's most powerful diesel. *Ian Allan Library*

differences in equipment and manufacture, the basic design was multiplied into several hundred units, some of which remain in service today as Class 218.

The 'V320'

During the years 1960-2 Henschel, in collaboration with DB, produced a further prototype, the C-C No V320, which began running at the beginning of 1963. The configuration was two 2,000hp powertrains, giving an overall power of 4,000hp. The choice of engine fell to the Daimler-Benz MB839Bb 16-cylinder machine, rated at 2,000hp at 1,475rpm; the transmission included a Voith L218rV torque-converter and a twin-gear-ratio arrangement. The top speed in the high-gear range was 100mph.

Six similar locomotives, equipped with Maybach MD870 engines and Voith L830rU transmissions, were supplied subsequently to the USA. One of them was tested in Germany before it was shipped, with its rating reduced to 3,800hp. Its weight was also reduced to 133 tons, to comply with German axle-load limits, whereas in the USA it was to be 148 tons. The maximum drawbar pull was 90,000lb at 2½mph in the low-gear range.

The 'V200¹s'

The 4,000hp 'V320' prototype was taken over by DB and ran until 1975, but it did not form the basis for a new class, owing to progressive electrification removing the need for diesel locomotives of such high power. Instead DB chose to stick with the 'V200'

The 2,700hp 'V200¹' class used the 'V200' body and bogies, ensuring continuity of the family resemblance. Here No V200.107 approaches Lindau on 5 August 1964 with the 'Rhône–Isar' express between Munich and Geneva.
Brian Stephenson

mechanical parts but to substitute the intercooled Mercedes-Benz MB839Ab engine, delivering 2,700hp at 1,500rpm and supplied with K184 transmissions. The powertrain chosen was the lightest with which DB had experience, and this enabled the locomotive to be mounted on B-B bogies, with the overall weight being kept as low as possible at 81 tonnes (80 tons). The result was known as the 'V200[1]' class, of which a batch of 20 was built by Krauss-Maffei, and the first was delivered to DB in late 1962. The maximum service speed was 87mph, and the calculated maximum and continuous tractive effort were respectively 55,000 and 50,000lb, both at 14.3mph. The class was later expanded to a total of 50, some of which remained in service well into the 1980s.

Service experience

Modern Railways for May 1965 gave some useful information about DB diesel performance. DB used a definition of a failure substantially different from that of British Railways, with a locomotive either being unable to start or complete its booked duty as the criterion. (According to BR a failure was any mechanical fault that caused a delay of five minutes to the final arrival time of a passenger service, or 10 minutes in the case of a freight train.) For the 'V200s', with all 86 in traffic by 1960, the average annual mileage during the period 1960-4 was 230,000km (140,000 miles), hauling an average trailing load of 340 tons.

Problems with the Voith transmission caused a drop in reliability from 2,000,000km (1,250,000 miles) in 1959 to 920,000 (570,000 miles) in 1960 and 375,000km (230,000 miles) in 1961. The performance returned to 2,000,000km (1,250,000 miles) by 1963. Overall reliability for the class was 190,000km (120,000 miles) in 1964, the recently introduced 'V200[1]' approaching 250,000km (150,000 miles) per annum. Several 'V200' Voith and Mekydro drives had successfully run 700,000-850,000km (435,000-530,000 miles) without needing to be opened up.

Turning to the MD650 engines, in the 1950s the interval between piston lifts was 300,000km (910,000 miles), but by 1965 this had been pushed up to between 400,000 and 450,000km (250,000 and 280,000 miles); indeed, several had accumulated between 500,000 and 800,000km (310,000 and 500,000 miles) without being removed from the locomotive. In 1963 the average mileage run between the general overhauls carried out that year was 615,000km (380,000 miles).

During early service the secondary drive on the prototype 'V160' locomotives gave trouble, but this was rectified before construction of the production series.

Turkish State Railways

Voith lost out in the choice of transmission for the 2,700hp Class V200[1], but the company did win an order for three sets of its L630r torque-converter in 'U' configuration for Turkey; this was the first order for the company's new triple-converter range of L630 and L830. The last character denoted the location of the output shaft; in its British Railways application, the transmission was the 'V' variant. Two Maybach MD655 diesels of 1,350hp at 1,500rpm were fitted, and the transmission was geared for 62mph. The maximum tractive effort at 30% adhesion was given as 73,200lb, and the continuous value was 59,400lb at 10.6mph, equivalent to 1,680rhp. Krauss-Maffei built the three locomotives, which had a centre cab and C-C wheel arrangement and were delivered in 1961. Before shipment, trials over the Black Forest route produced a speed of 35½mph up a gradient of 1 in 54 with 335 tons behind, which suggests around 2,000rhp.

7

MODERNISING BRITISH RAILWAYS' MOTIVE POWER

From 1948 the BTC comprised the publicly owned docks and harbours, waterways and road-haulage activities as well as British Railways. Within the BTC, British Railways was run by the Railway Executive.

The modernisation of British Railways motive power can be traced back to December 1948, when the BTC asked the Railway Executive to examine the balance of advantage between different forms of traction and to advise as to the nature of such large-scale experiments as were thought necessary to establish the economic facts. A committee of four was set up, comprising an administrator, two operators and an accountant, who took evidence from scientific and technical sources. It was not until October 1951 that a report emerged, recommending a pilot scheme of electrification, a large-scale trial of 2,000hp diesels, investigation of a scheme for a fleet of diesel multiple-units, and a massive expansion of the number of diesel shunters. Evidence of practice in both North America and Continental Europe had convinced the committee of the benefits that could be derived from the replacement of steam.

A programme for the acquisition of 573 shunters rated at 350hp and 141 of between 150 and 200hp, to be delivered between 1953 and 1957, had already been sanctioned by the Railway Executive, effectively a continuation of the work of the pre-nationalisation companies. A working party was set up to consider further the idea of multiple-units and reported during March 1952. It recommended nine areas for trials, Leeds/Bradford, Lincolnshire and West Cumbria being identified as priorities. Estimated costs per mile (including capital charges) were 2s 2½d (11p) for diesel and 7s 2½d (36p) for steam power. Again, the recommendations were taken up, as will be described in more detail in Chapter 9.

By October 1951 R. A. Riddles, the Engineering Member of the Railway Executive, had already embarked on a programme of building new steam locomotives, which incorporated the most modern design features. Riddles is said to have seen no benefit in an interim phase of main-line diesel traction between steam and large-

scale electrification, and in 1952 the Railway Executive effectively vetoed the BTC committee's recommendation for a large-scale trial of 2,000hp diesels.

It is only fair to note here that the transition from steam to electric traction for the main line envisaged by Riddles was a model adopted to a greater or lesser degree in several Continental countries, notably France and Italy. Even in West Germany, the DB never ordered more than about 140 diesel locomotives of 2,000hp or above, preferring to electrify the principal routes. A further factor in Britain during the early 1950s was a shortage of foreign exchange with which to buy oil overseas, whereas domestic coal was plentiful and cheap at the time.

A change of government brought a review in 1953 of the BTC structure, and the Railway Executive was abolished. New area boards (usually referred to as the 'regions') were set up, reporting to the BTC's General Staff, which was supported by its Central Staff. The new government was willing to fund railway modernisation, not least in order to make the system profitable. With the abolition of the Railway Executive Riddles retired as its Engineering Officer, thus removing an obstacle to large-scale use of main-line diesels. The General Staff (the BTC chairman and Commission members) decided to allocate a sizeable part of the modernisation funding to a main-line diesel programme, because this was viewed as offering a 'quick win' in terms of improved efficiency.

It can therefore be seen that, just as evidenced in Chapter 1, the migration from steam was primarily on economic grounds. Because of Riddles' opposition to large diesels beyond those commissioned by the LMS and Southern Railways, British experience at the time was limited to just Nos 10000 and 10001 and Nos 10201 and 10202 (those four with diesel-electric transmission) and No 10100 (with a mechanical transmission through differential gears and fluid couplings); No 10203 had yet to be completed. The experiment with gas-turbine power on the Western Region had not proved a success in terms of operating economy. Meanwhile, as already described, something was stirring in West Germany, and, although Britain was an island, the railway press kept engineers up to date with overseas developments.

The Modernisation Plan

At its meeting on 14 April 1954 the BTC set up a Planning Committee to prepare what was to be called the Modernisation Plan. The committee was composed of representatives both from the General and Central Staff and from the Area Boards. A subcommittee was formed to consider motive power, and had the following remit: (*a*) electrification of the majority of the main lines was ruled out, since money, time and staff would not be available, beyond lines that carried a certain traffic density; (*b*) if the Planning Committee could put forward reasonable justification on the basis of reports dealing with the performance of those diesels that the BTC already possessed, and such other reports as might be available to them, the BTC would be prepared to look sympathetically at a proposal for a bold programme for the trial of diesel locomotives.

By 11 August it was agreed that diesel power offered advantages over steam, but the issue of the balance of advantage of diesel versus electric remained open. The comparative costs of a British Railways Class 7 steam locomotive and a 2,000hp diesel-electric (the first use of this term in the official papers) found that for annual mileages above 40,000, the cost advantage lay with diesel. This assumed a 28% saving in repair costs, but the view was that experience with shunting locomotives did not bear this out, and that the break-even point was probably at 70,000 miles, which some 400 steam locomotives had achieved during 1952.

A meeting of the Planning Committee on 9 September, attended by the Chief of General Services (BTC) and Chief Regional General Managers, considered a report dated 4 June and agreed that the Western Region should submit a proposal for all diesel working in a selected area, and that the other regions should consider similar proposals. What the Western Region put forward was the elimination of all steam working west of Newton Abbot and the use of diesel locomotives based in that area for hauling a large proportion of the passenger and freight traffic from the West to London and Bristol; 105 main-line diesels were to displace 191 steam locomotives.

Meanwhile both the BTC Technical Research & Development Committee and the Works & Equipment Committee had been considering the options for transmissions for main-line diesels. Both of these committees were chaired by J. C. L. Train of the General Staff (a civil engineer), and their members comprised other General Staff members, Regional General Managers or Area Board chairmen and Central Staff heads of department, such as civil, electrical and mechanical engineering. It is clear that the BTC engineers were aware of the pilot scheme under way on the DB comprising the 'V80' and 'V200' types. R. C. Bond, by now British Railways' CME and so a part of the BTC's Central Staff, had produced a memorandum dated 29 September for the Works & Equipment Committee meeting of 6 October, and this was also discussed by the Technical Committee at its meeting on 14 November. By virtue of the considerable significance of its contents, the document is reproduced here in full.

This submission did not find unanimous support. Bond's opposite number on the Central Staff, the CEE, S. B. Warder, was not in agreement with Bond's arguments in favour of diesel-hydraulic; nor was Dr F. Q. den Hollander, Chairman of the Board of Nederlandse Spoorwegen (Netherlands Railways), who had been appointed to the Technical Committee as an external adviser. Den Hollander was an engineer and an advocate of electric traction, and had led the postwar rebuilding of his country's railways. Despite disagreeing with Bond's arguments, Warder and den Hollander concurred with

DIESEL LOCOMOTIVES WITH HYDRAULIC TRANSMISSION

Although, with the exception of the Fell Locomotive operating on the London Midland Region, only electric transmission has so far been fitted to diesel locomotives of over 500hp for British Railways, considerable development has taken place abroad in hydraulic transmission, notably in Germany, where the present policy is to use it in locomotives up to the highest powers in preference to electric transmission.

In this country up to date experience with hydraulic transmission in diesel locomotives is so far confined to eight 200hp light shunting locomotives, ordered from the North British Locomotive Co. Three of these locomotives, which have the German Voith torque-converter transmission made under licence by the North British Locomotive Co, are in service on the North Eastern Region and five more are now under construction for the Scottish Region.

Towards the end of last year, the North British Locomotive Co completed some mixed traffic locomotives, each of 625hp with hydraulic transmission, for the Mauritius Government Railways. A number of test runs, with both passenger and freight trains, were carried out on the Scottish Region, at one of which I was present. On that occasion two units coupled together worked passenger trains between Glasgow and Edinburgh in a most satisfactory manner.

More recently, the Firm have completed preliminary designs and specifications for locomotives in the higher power ranges, which would be suitable for service in this country. I have had a number of informal discussions concerning them with the North British Locomotive Co, who, with a view to assisting their export business, would like to see such locomotives running in regular service on British Railways.

While, as mentioned above, we are obtaining valuable experience with hydraulic transmission in low powered shunting locomotives, such experience is not necessarily valid for locomotives of higher powers. Having regard to the probable extension of diesel traction on British Railways it is, in my opinion, very desirable that trials should be made in this power range because of the potential advantages this form of transmission offers, which in relation to electric transmission could eventually be:

1. Reduced weight of locomotive for a given power
2. Lower first cost
3. Reduced maintenance costs

For such trials to be on a scale which would produce sufficient experience in a reasonably short time I suggest that five locomotives for mainline passenger and freight services in the 2,000hp range might be considered, together with six locomotives in the 1,000-1,250hp range to be used as twin units on heavy work or singly for lighter duties. The precise power characteristics to be selected will, of course be a matter for discussion with the Regions and with the Chief Officers concerned at Headquarters. Such locomotives would be suitable for service very widely throughout British Railways and could form part of any larger scheme involving the use of diesel electric locomotives also.

I therefore RECOMMEND that trials, as suggested above, should be carried out, and, as a first step, approval in principle is sought for the matter to be developed further with the North British Locomotive Co with a view to proposals and estimates of costs being obtained after which I would propose to make a further submission to this Committee.

[Signed] *R. C. Bond*

the proposal for a trial of this type of transmission. As a result the Works & Equipment Committee gave agreement in principle to Bond's proposals.

At the Technical Committee meeting on 23 September Bond and Western Region General Manager K. W. C. Grand were charged with looking into the possibility of bringing a German 'V200' to Britain, but on 14 November Bond explained that gauge restrictions ruled this out. At the same time he proposed that, in late January 1955, he and a party comprising E. S. Cox (his deputy), H. H. Phillips (Assistant General Manager, Western Region) and R. A. Smeddle (Western Region CME) should undertake a fact-finding trip to West Germany; the party also included representatives of NBL. Visits were actually made to DB and to Krauss-Maffei, Voith, MAN and other manufacturers. In truth, importing a 'V200' locomotive complete would have been politically unacceptable at the time, as emerged in 1955 when the Western Region proposed building a version with German-built engines and transmissions.

At the time of the visit, in January 1955, there were five 'V200s' in traffic, though none of these had MAN engines or Voith transmission. Later reports refer to DB, in particular, being coy about the performance of its main-line diesels; but the visitors agreed that the few examples then at work were 'certainly operating a railway', which was the phrase used by Cox in describing his conclusions on the visit. A key to the successful operation of the DB's locomotives was the use of a very limited number of carefully trained drivers.

Arising from the visit, on 17 February 1955 the BTC awarded a contract to NBL, in line with Bond's proposal of the previous September, for five 2,000hp and six 1,000hp locomotives at a total value of £720,000. The minutes of the Works Committee meeting on 23 March gave a breakdown of the contract value as five 2,000hp locomotives costing £430,000, six 1,000hp locomotives £318,000 and major spare parts £20,365, the actual total thus being £768,365.

This order was months ahead of the others placed under the BR Pilot Scheme, which were not made until October 1955. It also mirrored the German pilot scheme, which also involved 1,000hp and 2,000hp locomotives. The order to NBL was based on that company's proposals and quotes submitted to the BTC in 1953. What is interesting is that Bond had started a dialogue with NBL nearly a year before, without saying anything about it at any of the BTC committees' meetings, at least as far as the minutes record. At this time, although he was the British Railways CME within the Central Staff, Bond was two grades below BTC General Staff for Commission.

The surviving official files do not make clear just when the decision was taken to assign the 11 Pilot Scheme diesel-hydraulics from NBL to the Western Region. Brian Reed (a qualified engineer, a frequent contributor on hydraulic-transmission matters to the *Railway Gazette* and a member of the Institution of Locomotive Engineers) states that the Western Region undertook a study of the diesel-hydraulic concept during 1955 and that this was led by its Chairman, R. F. Hanks (appointed in 1955) and General Manager, K. W. C. Grand, the detail work being carried out by Grand's assistant, H. H. Phillips.

While this may be so, it is clear from the minutes of the Technical Committee that the decision to concentrate the 11 NBL locomotives on the Western Region had been taken at least as early as September 1954, because Messrs Bond and Grand were charged with examining whether a 'V200' could be brought to England. Cox was in a position to know how the decision to try the NBL locomotives on the Western Region was reached. He has written that the Western Region had no experience of electric transmission, and that the use of hydraulic transmission would avoid the need to enlarge its electrical side, which 'led them to welcome the suggestion that they should have the proposed diesel-hydraulic locomotives'. So it was not the Western Region's idea but that of the BTC Central Staff, a further reversal of what has hitherto been understood to have been the case. In fact, the Western Region *did* have a very limited experience of electric transmission, albeit in the shape of the two gas-turbine locomotives.

Left: The first order for diesel-hydraulics under the Pilot Scheme went to NBL for 11 locomotives, comprising six Type 2s and five Type 4s. The Type 2 design was subsequently favoured with orders for a further 52 locomotives, of which Nos D6316 and D6328 are seen leaving Truro with a westbound freight in June 1963.
D. C. Adams

The foregoing sets out a position that is at considerable variance with all the previous writings on this subject. These latter rely on Brian Reed's book on the WR diesel-hydraulics, in which he argues that the BTC Central Staff was grudging in its support for diesel-hydraulics and only gave the order to NBL as a sop to the Western Region. Clearly,

the official record presents a totally different picture, with the idea for main-line diesel-hydraulics coming from the Central Staff, not the Western Region, and that this interest dated from late 1953, when the first approach was made to NBL, not from 1955. Was this on the strength of the first press reports about the 'V200s' that were published in the last

Left: No D6321 awaits its next tour of duty as main-line pilot to Plymouth from Newton Abbot in July 1960.
D. C. Adams

As yet unnamed,
No D601 looks quite
bruised, but still new,
inside the new
maintenance shed at
Swindon.
Rail Photoprints

quarter of 1953? We shall never know, but, if not, the timing was highly coincidental! Note also that NBL invited Bond to participate in the pre-delivery main-line trials of its two diesel-hydraulic locomotives for Mauritius during January 1954.

A Western Region proposal

During March 1955 Grand received an offer from Maybach for the supply free of charge of two powertrains, each comprising the 1,000hp MD650 engine and Mekydro K104 transmission, to be fitted into a 2,000hp locomotive. Whether this offer was a reaction to the negotiations with NBL for MAN/Voith-equipped machines is not known, or whether it flowed from the visit to Germany in late January by Phillips and Bond, is not known; the record states only that Maybach made an offer to the Western Region. Whether the Western Region had asked Maybach to make such an offer is not recorded.

The big stumbling-block here was the import of German machinery, because, unlike MAN and Voith products, there was no British licensee for Maybach. The Western Region clearly appreciated this, and the

BTC's reluctance to extend the diesel-hydraulic trial to include a 'V200'-type machine built at Swindon with a German powertrain, and asked Maybach about the granting of a manufacturing licence to one or more British companies.

In a memorandum of 20 April Grand informed the Works Committee meeting on 23 May 1955 that he had received a cable from the Maybach company in the following terms:

Negotiations re transmissions with reputable firm have reached mutual basic agreement for co-operation, thus expecting early conclusion licence contract. First contacts concerning engine licence also established. As contemplated participation of Swindon in such production has bearing on both licensees, would appreciate to know whether our proposals for trial locomotive acceptable provided licence question settled to your satisfaction and extent of participation Swindon fixed.

In other words, the situation was becoming circular. The BTC wanted manufacture of German equipment to be undertaken by British licensees, but British companies were unwilling to become licensees without some prospect of a flow of orders from Swindon. In the light of the progress towards identifying a British licensee, the Committee recommended that the matter should be included on the agenda for the full BTC meeting on 26 May. The minutes of that meeting record that consideration was given to a submission of the Western Region Area Board, recommending the purchase of three sets of diesel engines and transmissions from Maybach for the sum of £126,000, as part and in advance of the 1957 locomotive building programme, so that three locomotives with hydraulic transmission might be constructed at Swindon Works (the 'Swindon Three'). The proposal was approved subject to acquisition being from the British licensee of Maybach. A rider was added that, so far as the BTC was concerned, 'In arranging for the construction at Swindon, it must be made clear that the work is of an experimental character and does not carry any commitments for the future.'

Specific reference was made to publicity because the BTC was extremely concerned about the public relations impact of a nationalised body buying German equipment a mere 10 years after the end of World War 2. Progress in resolving the licensing issue was slow, and the BTC minutes for the meeting on 22 September record:

Locomotive Build & Breaking up Programme 1957 — with reference to minute 8.250, Mr Bond, who attended for this item, outlined the position reached with Maybach and the expected difficulties in purchasing through British licensees. It was agreed if they could not be overcome quickly, the WR should arrange to purchase direct. The Public Relations adviser should keep in touch with this matter and if the purchase was from Germany, any publicity must indicate the efforts made to buy through a British agent.

Eventually Maybach agreed terms with Bristol Siddeley (part of the same group of companies as Brush Electrical Equipment Ltd) for granting a licence for the manufacture of diesel engines and with J. Stone for Mekydro transmission. Then, during 1956, the BTC entered into negotiations with Krauss-Maffei for a licence for its design of mechanical parts used in the DB 'V200s'. Meanwhile, on 23 February 1956, the BTC gave approval for the 'Swindon Three', at a cost of £107,625 each.

Summarising the above, in March 1955 Maybach offered a set of powertrains for a 2,000hp locomotive, but the Western Region wanted the trial of this equipment to be in three prototypes, not just one. Having got outline approval, the stumbling-block was the lack of a British licensee to manufacture the powertrain components. This dragged on during most of 1955 and explains in part why the announcement of the 'Swindon Three' did not come until 1956. The other part of the delay in making the announcement was the sensitivity, in the BTC's view, towards British Railways buying German equipment.

Between 14 November 1954 and 23 May 1955 the official minutes are silent with regard to the idea of trying a 'V200'-type machine in Britain, and this rules out being definitive now about anything that might have been going on behind the scenes. Cox is vague as to the source of the initiative to build the 'Swindon Three', and probably the only reliable publicly available record today can be

No D800 under construction at Swindon Works on 15 September 1957. *Ian Allan Library*

On 25 February 1959 the up and down workings of the 'Cornish Riviera Express' cross at Parsons Tunnel, Dawlish, hauled respectively by representatives of the 'D600' and 'D800' classes. *R. W. Stickling*

found in a paper read by G. E. Scholes, the head of the Swindon Drawing Office at the time, to the Institution of Locomotive Engineers on 17 November 1959. Referring to the 'V200s' and their high power-to-weight ratio, he commented that the Western Region proposed that a few similar locomotives should be built for trial in Britain in addition to those to be produced by NBL.

In conclusion, the origins of the trial of diesel-hydraulic drive have been set out above as fully and definitively as possible from the minutes of the relevant BTC papers, and this account gives a revisionist view of these events. The design implications of the policy decisions will be explored in the next chapter.

Pilot Scheme diesel-electrics

At its meeting on 11 November 1954 the Works Committee discussed the proposal to order 140 locomotives as part of a Pilot Scheme. These were all to be equipped with diesel-electric transmission and were to comprise 20 locomotives of Type A (later Type 1), 100 of Type B (later Type 2) and 20 of Type C (later Type 4), of which 20 Type Bs and 10 Type Cs were to be built in British Railways' own workshops. It was agreed to increase to 40 the number of Type A locomotives, making 160 in total. The minutes record 'disappointment' with the performance of the existing main-line diesels — a rather telling commentary on the designs.

At the BTC meeting of 17 February 1955 approval was given to the ordering of 10 Type A locomotives from English Electric for the Eastern Region and 10 from British Railways'

works for the London Midland, as part of the 1956 Locomotive Building Programme. The meeting of 24 March gave authority under the 1957 and 1958 programmes for the construction of 140 locomotives. By the time of the meeting of the Works Committee on 29 September tenders from 16 companies had been evaluated, of which 11 were from Britain, and these gained BTC approval to become the Locomotive Pilot Scheme within the Modernisation Plan.

Of the locomotives ordered, 10 of the Type Bs were to come from English Electric and to have a Deltic engine of 1,100hp. This comes as no surprise in the light of the discussion held by the Technical Committee at its December 1954 meeting, referred to in Chapter 2. Twenty further Type Bs were to have a two-stroke engine, in order to assess this against the traditional British four-stroke type. The General Motors 567 range for rail traction was a two-stroke engine and was achieving considerable production volume both in the USA and around the world, but at this time British Railways felt it sensible to try out a 'standard' two-stroke of British design; of course, the Deltic engine operated on a two-stroke cycle, but this was a specialised design.

From the standpoint of this book, the orders of most interest were 10 diesel-electric Type Bs from NBL and the 20 diesel-electric Type Cs. This is because the Type Bs were to be identical to the six diesel-hydraulic Type Bs already sanctioned, except for the transmission. It was said at the time that this would facilitate a direct comparison between the two forms of transmission. Turning to the Type Cs, 10 of them were, effectively, to replicate No 10203 (apart from some external differences) and were to be designed and built by English Electric. The other 10 were to come from BR's Derby Works and to have a Sulzer diesel and Crompton Parkinson electrical machines. Within the Pilot Scheme, British Railways therefore had two Type Bs identical except for transmission, and four designs of Type C — two diesel-electric and two diesel-hydraulic, the latter comprising one with traditional mechanical construction and one based on 'V200' mechanical parts. Detailed consideration of these designs follows in the next chapter.

Above: With the stated intention of comparing diesel-electric and diesel-hydraulic drive, the BTC ordered a diesel-electric version of the 'D6300' class from NBL as part of the Pilot Scheme. Initially based on the Eastern Region in the King's Cross area, the locomotives were quickly sent back to Scotland, ostensibly to be near the manufacturer for rectification. No doubt making its last journey on English soil, No D6138 leads EE Type 4 ('D200') No D259 over Relley Mill Viaduct, Durham, on 12 February 1960. *I. S. Carr*

Left: The BTC was keen to try a Type 2 with a Napier Deltic-type engine, ordering a batch of 10 locomotives as part of the Pilot Scheme. For various reasons they were unsuccessful. Allocated to outer-suburban and empty-stock diagrams from King's Cross, No D5901 is seen here with a rake of suburban stock. *Ian Allan Library*

Right: The Pilot Scheme involved five diesel-electric Type 2 designs. In addition to the 'Baby Deltic' (see Chapter 2) and NBL designs came BR's own offering, in the form of the 'D5000' class. Here a later example, No D5092, heads a fuel train for Marylebone DMU depot out of Canfield Tunnel, Finchley, on 21 May 1966. *I. S. Krause*

Below: The Birmingham Railway Carriage & Wagon Co Ltd supplied a Type 2 that proved to have some design advantages over its BR equivalent. It is represented here by Nos D5320 and D5328 as they climb through Bridge of Allan with a Glasgow Buchanan Street–Inverness train on 29 July 1964. *Derek Cross*

Left: Brush Electrical Engineering Co Ltd designed a Type 2 of considerably greater weight than those illustrated hitherto and had in consequence to use an A1A bogie rather than the two-axle Bo configuration. Here Nos D5645 and D5604 are in charge of empty-stock trains in the cutting outside King's Cross. *Ian Allan Library*

Below: The choice of a Type 2 with a two-stroke engine resulted in the Crossley-engined 'D5700s', built by Metropolitan-Vickers. Before their refurbishment the engine could frequently be seen smoking badly; No D5705 demonstrates the point as it climbs the 1-in-132 gradient past Disley on the ascent towards Peak Forest with the 12.25pm Manchester Central–Derby on 18 April 1959. *A. H. Bryant*

Above: No Type 1 diesel-hydraulic design was included in the Pilot Scheme. The diesel-electric offerings had a single cab, as shown here in this official view of British Thomson-Houston No D8200, still without BR emblem. *Ian Allan Library*

Right: All three of the Pilot Scheme Type 1 designs suffered from poor forward visibility when the nose end was leading. Illustrating the problem is this view of English Electric No D8127, setting off from Glasgow Central with a race special for Lanark. *Norman Pollock*

Above: Two Type 4 designs were ordered under the Pilot Scheme, one of from English Electric. This had had the same powertrain as Southern prototype No 10203. With electrification work in progress at Lichfield Trent Valley on 3 March 1962, No D370 pilots Stanier 'Black Five' No 45113 on the down 'Mid-Day Scot'. *Michael Mensing*

Left: It was rumoured that the Type 4 from BR Derby weighed over 140 tons, and it certainly took much longer to design and build than did the English Electric 'D200'. The Pilot Scheme locomotives were soon relegated to goods work; here No D8 *Penyghent* has charge of a rake of empty coal wagons at Shipley Gate, on the Erewash Valley line, on 2 September 1969. *J. S. Hancock*

8

A CONTRAST IN DESIGN

This chapter will look at the diesel-locomotive designs that emerged from 1954; how they fared will be reviewed in Chapter 10. First, however, it is worth bringing the General Motors story up to date, to show parallel developments in North America and because General Motors was invited — but declined — to respond to the BTC's Pilot Scheme tender. From January 1954 GM introduced the 'C' version of its 567 two-stroke engine. In 16-cylinder form it produced a gross output of 1,900hp at 835rpm, and this remained the rating in 1956. In other words, development in North America in terms of engine output by slow-speed engines was not ahead of comparable units in Britain and on the Continent.

The North British Locomotive Co Ltd

NBL was to play a key role in the diesel-hydraulic story, because the company held licences for German equipment, which meant that diesel-hydraulic transmissions could be manufactured in Britain at a time when direct importation from Germany was politically unacceptable. The following sets out the background to its involvement in this form of traction.

At the end of World War 2 NBL appreciated that railways in North America and in mainland Europe were taking steps to move away from steam traction. The company was, essentially, a 'metal-basher', lacking its own ranges of diesel engines and electrical machines. NBL therefore began to move towards diesel-locomotive production by acquiring the UK and Commonwealth licence to manufacture Voith diesel-hydraulic transmissions.

The first licensee for the Voith system for the British Empire had been the Hydraulic Coupling & Engineering Co Ltd of Isleworth, in 1934. By 1949 this licence had lapsed and been taken up by NBL. August 1951 witnessed the emergence of the first two shunting locomotives, equipped with a Davey Paxman 6RPH engine of 200hp at 1,000rpm and a Voith model L33y transmission; one locomotive operated in one of the NBL works in Glasgow, the other in a steelworks in Corby. The shunters had an 0-4-0 wheel arrangement and an overall weight of 32 tons.

In late 1953 the company unveiled its first main-line diesel-hydraulic locomotives — two 625hp machines for Mauritius. The design had to take special account of the steeply graded character of the route, which had a ruling gradient of 1 in 27. By coincidence, Sharp, Stewart & Co, NBL's predecessor, had supplied the first steam locomotives to the island. The Paxman 12RPHXL-II engine was rated at 625hp at 1,250rpm, though the site rating was 605hp by virtue of the climate and altitude. Coupled to this was a Voith L37zv hydraulic transmission, comprising a single-stage torque-converter and two fluid couplings, giving a three-stage transmission suitable for 45mph. These were the locomotives referred to by Bond in his memorandum to the Works & Equipment Committee of 23 September 1954 (see Chapter 7).

On 18 August 1954 MAN in Germany had concluded an agreement with NBL for the manufacture of diesel engines of up to 2,000hp for rail traction. MAN had built Rudolf Diesel's first engine in 1893. During the 1950s MAN produced low-, medium- and

The NBL diesel-hydraulic locomotive for Mauritius, which when demonstrated during trials in Scotland helped persuade R. C. Bond, the British Railways CME, to try this type of transmission on the main line in Britain. *North British Locomotive Co*

high-speed engines. The predecessor to the L12V18/21 used in the Pilot Scheme orders was the L12V17.5/21, which was rated at 1,000hp at 1,500rpm; it had been used in streamlined trains and railcars. An increase in cylinder bore of ½mm to 18mm in 1955 produced the engine used in Britain.

At the company's 1955 annual general meeting, the chairman boasted that NBL 'has in hand well over 100 diesel-hydraulic locos'. Sadly, this level of activity was to prove short-lived. Writing in *Diesel Railway Traction* in June 1963, Dr Carlos Knapp, at the time leading director of Voith Getriebe KG in Heidenheim, observed of NBL's performance:

> It was a difficult proposition to convert from that of steam locomotives to the much more exacting requirements of the production of highly developed diesel engines and hydraulic drives. Unfortunately, NBL did not succeed in introducing modern methods of the necessary width of range. Apart from the disappointment brought about by technical difficulties, the first diesel-hydraulic locomotives manufactured in Glasgow also proved to be a great financial loss.

For several reasons NBL entered creditors' voluntary liquidation on 19 April 1962.

Pilot Scheme designs

Perhaps the greatest distinction between prevailing construction practices can be observed in the two Pilot Scheme designs of diesel-hydraulic Type 4s, one of traditional construction and the other of monocoque type. These designs are dealt with in detail below.

The NBL Type 4s or 'D600s'

The NBL Type 4s were the five locomotives, together with six Type 2s, that were the subject of the British Railways enquiry in 1953 and for which purchase was sanctioned by the BTC during March 1955. At the time of No D600's introduction the Western Region issued a publicity booklet describing the locomotive, and it is useful here to refer to

its contents. The preamble makes clear that design and construction was to the BTC's general requirements, under the overall direction of Bond, the British Railways CME. Specific reference is made to Smeddle's having responsibility for the detailed design and construction of the locomotives (to be described later) to be built at Swindon.

The basic dimensions were: length 65ft, weight 117½ tons, driving-wheel diameter 3ft 7in, and maximum permitted speed 90mph. The British Railways Diagram Book quoted a maximum tractive effort of 49,460lb, which corresponds roughly to a 27½% factor of adhesion (see Chapter 5); the continuous rating was 39,600lb at 12.6mph.

The mainframe of the locomotive was constructed from mild steel plates and sections. Main longitudinal members were built up in traditional fashion to form an 'I' section and braced by cross-stretchers. Plates and channels completed the framework, on top of which the platform was built to form a continuous floor. Standard side buffers and drawgear were fitted at each end of the locomotive. To reduce weight, the cab nose ends were made of cast aluminium.

Bogie design was of the double-plate type with welded sub-assemblies, and had three axles, of which only the outer two were powered. Transverse, traction and braking forces were taken by an inner and outer centring ring; the inner part of the ring was attached to the locomotive underframe, while the outer part was integral with the bolster. The total weight of the locomotive's mainframe and superstructure was taken by four widely-spaced bearing pads, which rested on a double swing-link bolster. The bolster in turn rested on transverse laminated springs supported from the bogie frames by spring link planks and swing links. From the bogie frame, the load was transferred to the grease-lubricated Timken roller-bearing axleboxes by a system of beams and coil springs.

Power was supplied by two powertrains. Each comprised a MAN L12V18/21A 12-cylinder diesel and a Voith L306r torque-converter with cardan-shaft drive. Each engine had a Napier turbocharger and was rated at 1,000hp at 1,445rpm. The engine was mounted on a bedplate, which was mounted flexibly to the underframe. A Hardy-Spicer cardan shaft connected the engine output shaft to the torque-converter. Engine cooling was by a Serck Radiators Ltd radiator unit driven by a British Thomson-Houston electric motor, with one cooler group per engine.

Under prevailing Voith nomenclature, model L306r meant that the transmission was designed for locomotive applications, had three hydraulic circuits, no fluid couplings, was in power category 6, and had built-in reverse gears. Later this nomenclature was revised, with the power category digit first, then the number of torque-converters within the unit and finally the number of fluid couplings. As installed in the 'D600s', the maximum rating was an input of 925hp at 1,445rpm.

Drive from each transmission to the axle-mounted gearboxes was through Hardy-Spicer cardan shafts fitted with needle-bearing universal joints. The gearboxes on each bogie had spiral bevel reduction gears, and the reaction torque from each gearbox was taken through torque arms and rubber bushes to the

Built by the North British Locomotive Co at is Glasgow works, the original A1A-A1A 'Warship', No D600, is seen on trial in Scotland in December 1957. This locomotive would later be named *Active*.
Ian Allan Library

bogie frame. Each powertrain could operate independently of the other.

Each engine had a dynostarter driven directly from the crankshaft. When acting as a generator this provided a 110V electrical supply for auxiliaries and battery-charging. When acting as a starter motor, it drew current from the battery.

The BTC engaged the Design Research Unit to advise on external styling, while NBL engaged a design consultant for both the Type 4s and for Type 2s. Although NBL wished to retain as much commonality as possible between the two designs, this did not prove a practical proposition with regard to the nose-end styling of the smaller locomotives.

NBL was under the impression that Standard Locomotive Green was to be applied all over the body, but the Design Research Unit had other ideas. Eventually, mid-grey was used for the central roof section, and a thin light grey line was applied at solebar level between the cab doors. The locomotives were to be named after Royal Navy ships, and the nameplates were affixed as near the midpoint of the body as was possible.

The Swindon Type 4s or 'D800s'

The Swindon Type 4 design was the one that the works derived from the Krauss-Maffei 'V200' class — 'derived' because the latter was 10in taller and 16in wider than was permissible within the British loading-gauge, and had some undergear equipment that required modification. Although only three locomotives were sanctioned initially as part of the Pilot Scheme, a further 30 were ordered on 28 February 1957; together they were numbered D800-32. Five more were ordered on 9 April 1959; they were numbered D866-70. They were highly significant machines because of the method of construction used, its first application in a British main-line diesel locomotive. Opportunity has therefore been taken here to refer to sections of a paper presented to the Institution of Locomotive Engineers during 1959 by G. E. Scholes, the head of the Swindon Drawing Office, about the design; given the precepts of the design of superstructure later becoming adopted widely in Britain, his comments on this method of assembly are also worth noting.

The overall length was 60ft, the weight in working order 78½ tons, and the maximum tractive effort 48,600lb, with a continuous rating of 46,900lb at 11½mph; top speed was 90mph.

The class had two Maybach MD650 12-cylinder 'V'-form engines installed, each developing 1,135hp at 1,530rpm (except for Nos D800-2, in which the engines were set to develop 1,056hp at 1,400rpm). No D830 was fitted with two Paxman 12YJXL Ventura units, rated at 1,135hp at 1,530rpm, in place of the two MD650s. Power was transmitted to both axles of each four-wheel bogie through a Mekydro K.104 transmission, as developed by Maybach; the transmission was secured to the underframe of the locomotive and occupied the centre portion of the pivotless bogie designed by Krauss-Maffei to accommodate such a transmission.

In designing the 'V200' locomotives the Germans adopted a lightweight construction technique whereby thin plate, appropriately stiffened, was enabled to withstand the loading imposed on it. This technique, based on theoretical work by Timoshenko dating

Cross-country services between the West of England and the North West were routed via the Welsh Marches, with a traction change at Shrewsbury until the electrification of the West Coast main line moved it to Crewe. In steam days these turns were shared between Newton Abbot and Shrewsbury sheds, but the advent of the 'D800s' saw the new order take over all these diagrams. A busy scene at Pontrilas on 27 June 1963 finds freights stabled in the loops on the busy North & West line as No D800 *Sir Brian Robertson* powers south with 12 carriages forming the 9.05am from Liverpool Lime Street. *A. A. Vickers*

back to 1921, was developed after extensive research in the spheres of aircraft and steel building construction, and was later applied successfully to coach design.

In use, the technique involved a tentative method of approach, a structure having to be assumed in the first place and loads estimated. Diagrams showing shear force and polar bending moment were set out, and for this purpose the weights of the main components were assumed to act at their centre of gravity, while the weights of the auxiliary equipment and of the underframe and body were assumed to be equally distributed over the length of the locomotive. At any particular section of the locomotive the shear force and bending moment depends upon the manner in which the structure is carried or lifted. The following cases had to be considered:

1. Normal loading, that is, with the body supported at the bogie centres
2. Lifting the whole locomotive, including the bogies, at the lifting points provided, which were symmetrical about the locomotive centre
3. Lifting the body and one bogie at a buffer beam with the bogie centre furthest from the beam acting as a fulcrum
4. Lifting at both buffer beams

Diagrams were drawn for all these conditions; then a series of lengthy calculations were made for various sections along the locomotive, to determine not only the strength of the section as a whole but also the buckling strength of every unsupported area of plate forming part of the load-carrying skin of the superstructure. If, in the outcome, the proposed arrangement proved to be too weak or unnecessarily strong, it had to be modified to a second approximation and the calculations repeated.

For each section of the locomotive, the calculations followed the same pattern. First, the moments of inertia of each frame-member section and each plate section, including the body skin, were determined, the sum of these giving the moment of inertia of

the whole cross-section. Using the highest of the bending moments resulting at this cross-section from the various methods of loading, the maximum tensile and compressive bending stresses were then calculated. The bending stresses due to normal loading were also derived, and were multiplied by a factor of 1.3 to allow for dynamic loading. The maximum shearing stress, and the compressive stress in the underframe alone due to a buffing load of 200 tons, were also calculated.

The horizontal and vertical members of the body framing divided the skin into unsupported rectangular sections, which, in the calculation of the bending and shearing stresses for the whole cross-section, were assumed to be rigid. The technique involved was that described previously as having been developed in Germany. Formulae were used that took into account the size of the plate, its ratio of length to width, and its thickness. For each rectangle of plate through which the particular section of the locomotive under consideration passed, permissible buckling stresses for the shear load and for the compressive load were calculated, except for those plates in tension, for which it was necessary only to calculate a shear buckling stress. The actual shear and compressive buckling stresses were then calculated for each method of loading, and compared with those considered permissible. A formula involving the permissible and actual values of both kinds of buckling stress was then used to calculate a 'factor of safety'.

It is of interest to note in passing that, unlike the behaviour of columns, in which loading in excess of the critical loading causes complete collapse, in the type of construction under consideration the immediate result of such buckling is limited to a shift of stresses from the part concerned to adjacent parts of the structure. The limiting 'factor of safety' was therefore unity. An interesting sidelight on this was provided by a test, carried out by Krauss-Maffei, in which a 'V200' locomotive was lifted at the buffer beams. One of the skin plate sections had a 'factor of safety' of something less than one, and it was said that this particular plate could be observed to deform under load but that it returned to its normal shape when the load was removed, which served to illustrate the soundness of the theory.

The buckling safety factors apply only if the buckling stresses do not exceed the elastic limit of the material, in this case mild steel. A maximum resultant buckling stress was therefore calculated for each plate and multiplied by the 'factor of safety', the result being compared with the allowable stress, for which a value of 13 tons per square inch was used in the 'D800' application.

Finally, normal methods of calculation were applied to examine the strength as struts of the various horizontal cantrail and body frame members. The essential parts of this structure were two solid-drawn steel tubes of 6½in outside diameter and 0.192in thickness running in a single length from one end of the locomotive to the other. A number of lateral plate members ⁵⁄₃₂in thick were threaded onto these tubes to form, with longitudinal plates of the same thickness, a honeycomb-like underframe to which the ⁵⁄₃₂in-thick decking plate was fixed. The superstructure consisted of a light framework of 0.104in-thick bent steel sections covered with 0.080in-thick steel plate. The whole was welded together and thoroughly cleaned before being painted with primer.

The bogies of this locomotive were of considerable interest, in that the normal axlebox-in-guide type of construction was not used, and there was no bolster and no centre pivot. The weight of the superstructure was carried by the buckles of the laminated springs through which it was transferred to the bogie frame by way of spring hangers, coil springs and frame brackets. The pads resting on the tops of the coil springs were immediately beneath pads affixed to the superstructure, but were separated from it by a distance of ¹⁵⁄₁₆in. The bogie frame was carried on four laminated springs, which in turn transferred the weight to the four axlebox housings and thence through self-aligning Skefko roller bearings to the axles. The housings were integral with arms that were pivoted at their inner ends to the mainframe by long rubber-bushed bearings, thus eliminating the need for axlebox liners and horns, and thereby avoiding the wear normally associated with such parts.

The bogie frame was constrained to pivot about its geometrical centre by the Krauss-Maffei patent linkage consisting of two bellcranks carried in brackets on the bogie frame, a link connecting the laterally disposed arms of the bellcranks, and two links connecting the longitudinal arms to brackets secured to the superstructure. Each of the eight pins in this linkage was carried in substantial rubber bearing bushes. Traction and braking forces were transmitted from the bogies directly to the superstructure, the surface of each pad being part of a cylinder, and that of each pad part of a sphere. These pads were of manganese steel.

The wheel diameter was 3ft 3½in, and this, with an axle load of 19 tons 13cwt, gave a P/D ratio (see page 19) of 5.97. This was in excess of the ratio of 5 originally calculated on purely theoretical grounds as the limit beyond which Hertzian stresses would become troublesome, but in view of the almost insurmountable difficulties in this design of reducing the ratio to such a low value, the figure was allowed to remain at 5.97. It was common knowledge that the limitations imposed by the Civil Engineer were often contrary to the interests of the locomotive engineer, and in the matter of Hertzian stresses it may well be that even if a P/D ratio as low as 5 was necessary to safeguard the track completely, the imposition of such a figure would not in the long run have proved to be economic.

At the date of the paper the question of the relative merits of high-speed and low-speed diesel engines for railway use was still a controversial issue among locomotive engineers. The high-speed engine was attractive in that it was smaller and lighter than its low-speed counterpart, but it was still held by many that the low-speed engine was more reliable and needed less maintenance. The Maybach MD range of high-speed engines was the result of many years of development with a view to achieving parity in these respects with their low-speed rivals.

The outstanding feature of the MD range was the so-called 'tunnel' design of the crankcase. Each pair of crank webs and the associated journal of an orthodox design were replaced by one large disc. Each disc carried a roller-type main bearing of large diameter, the outer race of which was mounted on the transverse walls of the crankcase. The crankcase was in one piece, forming, as it were, a tunnel, into which the crankshaft was introduced from one end. The great advantage of this design was that it made available practically the whole length of the crankshaft for main and connecting rod bearings, and this in turn enabled the cylinders to be set close together, thus shortening the engine and giving maximum crankshaft rigidity, while still leaving ample provision for the bearings. The connecting rods were of the fork-and-blade type.

The pistons were cooled by a continuous flow of oil, and this enabled piston clearances to be reduced to a very small amount. The piston heads, which were bolted to the piston bodies for ease of removal at overhauls, were of alloy steel and carried the compression rings. These features improved efficiency and resulted in a low rate of piston wear.

Right: The production-series 'D800' ('Warship') locomotives were ordered as part of the Western Region's 'dieselisation' programme for the lines west of Newton Abbot, taking in through services to/from London. Here No D868 *Zephyr* runs past Dawlish Warren with the down 'Cornish Riviera Express' on 25 June 1961. *M. Pope*

Right: Another named Western Region train, the 'Torbay Express', heads away from Westbury behind 'Warship' No D811 *Daring* on 28 April 1962. *G. A. Richardson*

The engine had individual detachable cylinder heads, each having three inlet and three exhaust valves arranged around the combustion chamber. This multiplicity of valves meant that each was small and therefore well cooled and lowly stressed. The valves were operated from overhead camshafts through the medium of rockers with hydraulic adjusters, which took up clearance automatically and made the valve gear run quietly.

A further interesting feature was the combination of a fuel-injection pump and fuel injector in a single unit. This unit was developed by L'Orange and Maybach to overcome the difficulties experienced with separate pumps and valves when used on large high-speed engines, these difficulties being due chiefly to the resistance of the necessary connecting pipes and their tendency to 'breathe', that is, fluctuate in capacity, under the high pressure in use. At the time of the paper in 1959 these injector units had proved to be highly satisfactory in service on the 'D800'-class locomotives.

The aforementioned design features, together with the use of the finest materials and an insistence on the highest standard of workmanship (in Germany), made possible an engine which, it was claimed, had none of the disadvantages usually associated with high speeds of revolution.

It should perhaps be mentioned that the first Maybach engines to be used in the construction of the 'D800' class were of German manufacture, but that Bristol Siddeley manufactured the remainder, under licence, at its Coventry works.

The cooling units were supplied by Serck Radiators Ltd and fitted with the Serck-Behr hydrostatic fan drive. The fan pump was driven directly from the engine, and circulated oil from the reservoir to the fan motor and back to the reservoir either directly or by way of a thermostatically operated controller. The amount of oil that was bypassed directly to the reservoir depended on the temperature of the engine cooling water, which therefore controlled the speed of the fan. The radiator shutters were actuated by a control cylinder, operated by oil tapped from the main pressure line, and the apparatus was arranged so that just before the fan started, the shutters began to open under the slowly increasing oil pressure. When the fan reached about a quarter speed, the shutters were fully opened. In effect, the fan speed was low and the shutters nearly closed when the cooling water temperature was low, so ensuring that the engine quickly reached its optimum working temperature. On the 'D800' class, the shutters began to open and the fan began to rotate when the cooling water reached a temperature of about 170°F, the normal working temperature being about 180°F; these temperatures were the same as on the 'D600s'. The engine was automatically stopped if the temperature reached 195°F. The main advantages claimed for the hydrostatic fan drive were as follows:

- The fan speed and shutter opening were governed automatically by the temperature of the coolant, hence the power consumption of the fan was no more than was necessary to maintain the most favourable coolant temperature
- Fuel consumption and engine wear were both reduced, because the optimum coolant temperatures were reached in the shortest possible time and maintained irrespective of load or ambient conditions
- The apparatus needed little maintenance, as all the moving parts ran in oil
- There was a saving in weight as compared with the electric fan drive used in the 'D600s'

Although not mentioned by Scholes, hydrostatic fan drives of this type were not without their own issues, a significant one being the difficulty of keeping the high-pressure system leaktight. It was feared at first that trouble might be experienced with seizure of the pumps and motors, which were identical units, as a result of dirt in the pipelines. Such trouble was, however, avoided by the meticulous cleaning of all pipes before and during erection. From experience gained previously it would seem that this type of fan drive, if properly assembled, was efficient and highly dependable.

The engine manufacturers recommended that engines should not be started with a coolant temperature of less than 104°F, and to comply with this requirement an oil-fired pre-heater was fitted in the cooling water circuit of each engine. This pre-heater, known as a Vapor-Watchman Heater and made by J. Stone & Co, of Deptford, was automatically controlled by the temperature of the cooling water, which was maintained between 135°F and 145°F when the engine was not running. The MAN engines used in the 'D600s' did not require such pre-heating. The advantages claimed for this installation were:

- The engine was kept warm and ready for easy starting and immediate operation at normal loads
- Continual expansion and contraction was minimised
- Oil dilution and sludge caused by the condensate formed in cold engines were minimised
- Wear in the cylinders was greatly reduced
- As there was no need to idle the engine to keep it warm, the saving in fuel oil helped to offset (and in some circumstances more than offset) the cost of running the pre-heater

As in the case of the engines, the first Mekydro K104 transmissions used for the 'D800' class were of German manufacture, but J. Stone & Co subsequently manufactured them under licence in England.

The axle drives, also of Maybach design, were of ample proportions and of robust build. The casing was of cast steel. The bevel wheels were spiral-toothed and the driving pinion was supported on straddle-mounted bearings, ensuring quiet running and accurate meshing of the teeth, with a minimum of deflection even under maximum torque loads. The axle drive was supported on the axle by large-diameter roller bearings. Lubrication of gearwheels and bearings was provided by a twin-gear-type oil pump incorporating an oil filter. The driving torque, passing through the axle drives, was counteracted by torque reaction arms that were resiliently suspended from the bogie frame.

The cardan-shaft layout, as designed for the 'V200' class, was adopted without any material changes. A good deal of investigation into the use of cardan shafts for high power appeared to have been undertaken in Germany, and it was felt that until considerable experience had been gained on British Railways, it was advisable not to depart from well-tried principles.

It need only be said here that, apparently, it was quite easy to mount the drive in such a way as to cause excessive torque irregularities, these in turn resulting in vibration of the shafts, which caused bad running and a much-reduced life. The point at issue was, of course, to determine how far one could safely depart, in the case of a coupling between two relatively moving parts like underframe and bogie, from the normal requirement of the double Hooke joint, which is that the angle between the driving shaft and the intermediate shaft was the same as the angle between the intermediate shaft and the driven shaft, and that all the shafts should be in the same plane. These issues were to haunt Swindon in relation to, in particular, the 'D1000s', to be described later.

Most of the electrical equipment was supplied by British Brown-Boveri Ltd, and was similar to that used on the 'V200' class. The following points, however, may be of some interest. Although the locomotives were diesel-hydraulics, about 2½ miles of wiring was required in each to couple up to the various electrical devices used for controlling and safeguarding the power units and for lighting circuits etc. There were many small electric motors to drive auxiliaries such as exhausters, compressor, oil pumps, controls for the train-heating boiler and pumps circulating cooling water.

The main engines were started electrically, each being connected via a 1:2.28 step-up gear, housed in the transmission casing, to a dynostarter located in the nearer nose end of the locomotive. The dynostarters when used as generators were rated at 110V, 150A, and supplied current for all electrical apparatus and for battery charging. The two machines worked together in parallel when both engines were running, or singly when one engine only was in use.

The system controlling engine speed was of the all-electric type and regulated the speed and (hence the power) in seven steps (six on the first three prototypes) as shown in the following table.

Controller notch	Engine speed (rpm)
0	600 (engine idling)
1	600 (engine driving)
2	950
3	1,140
4	1,275
5	1,370
6	1,460
7	1,530

Moving the controller from notch 0 to notch 1 caused the torque-converter turbine to engage, and the locomotive began to move with the engine or engines still running at 600rpm. Jumper connections enabled two or three 'D800s' (except Nos D800-2) to be worked in multiple.

Scholes' comments on external styling were illuminating. The external shape and decoration of a diesel locomotive seems to give rise to more argument and divergence of views than do any other elements of the design. Locomotive drawing offices were apt to be a little impatient over this matter, considering that, if left alone, they could probably have done as well as anybody else! In this, however, they were perhaps mistaken. There was already a growing tendency to leave the styling to specialists in this field, and as with the 'D600s', the Design Research Unit was asked by the BTC's Design Panel to undertake this part of the work.

Scope for originality in this direction was severely restricted by exigencies of technical design, itself largely influenced by the limitations imposed by the loading-gauge. However, very substantial differences in appearance could be achieved by the shaping of the end of the locomotive and the cab windows, and by the surface treatment of the exterior.

Close co-operation between the Design Research Unit and the Swindon staff at first

The lines of the German 'V200' are clearly evident in this view of Swindon's scaled-down version of the Krauss-Maffei design. No D870 *Zulu*, the last of the Swindon production run, enters Mutley Tunnel as it heads its train out of Plymouth bound for London on 30 April 1962. *Brian Haresnape*

'V200' lines are also clearly to the fore in this picture of an unidentified locomotive heading a lengthy train of vacuum-braked four-wheel vans at Barry Docks.
Ian Allan Library

resulted in the building of a ½in:1ft model embodying proposals which were promptly rejected by the management. Further efforts, based on directives given after the first proposals had been studied, resulted in a second model, which was declared to be of outstanding merit and was therefore acceptable!

There was no room for the usual prominent nose, which in the opinion of many was fortunate, but by careful attention to the contours and by causing the front and side cab windows to appear as a unified shape, an end of some distinction, it is considered, was achieved. The bodyside was continued downwards as a skirt wrapped under at a belt line, which was naturally created at 3ft 6in above rail level by the shape of the loading-gauge.

The final touches were the form and position of the locomotive name and number, the latter having been regarded as punctuating the painted-on horizontal line, and the separation of the roof area in grey paintwork, in contrast to the standard green of the body.

As part of its expansion of the Area 1 scheme, on 27 February 1957, in addition to ordering a further 30 'D800s' from Swindon, the Western Region was authorised to approach NBL with a view to NBL's producing locomotives with the Swindon/Krauss-Maffei mechanical parts but the same powertrain used in the NBL 'D600s'. Before concluding a contract with the BTC, NBL had to negotiate a licence with Krauss-Maffei. After tendering, the proposed quantity was reduced by one, to 33 locomotives. They were numbered D833-65.

The powertrain was an updated version of the MAN 12V18/21 engine in 'B' form, rated at 1,100hp at 1,530rpm, and the Voith LT306r hydraulic transmission. Of significance is a mention in the Swindon Works annual report for 1958, which stated that work on a batch of 30 'D800s' had been started and *the last 10* would be arranged to accept the MAN/Voith powertrain, if required, in addition to the Maybach/Mekydro variant that was the Swindon standard for the class; this was with a view to replicating the same interchangeability adopted by DB for 'V200' power equipment, but was, in the event, never used.

The foregoing explains several philosophies in the design. First, the mechanical parts of the 'D600s' built by NBL were entirely traditional, with a load-bearing underframe and P/D ratio in keeping with the Civil Engineer's diktat, causing the use of three-axle bogies with a

middle carrying-axle to reduce the loading. By contrast, the modern, German-inspired construction techniques employed in the 'D800s' produced a design on two-axle bogies, all powered, that was 5ft shorter and 29 tons lighter (equivalent to a coach). The NBL product employed a traditional design of bogie, whereas Swindon adopted one of Krauss-Maffei origin. Both had roughly the same adhesion weight, and so the same maximum tractive effort.

Even within the powertrain there were contrasts. The Maybach engine was more sophisticated than its MAN equivalent, bringing both benefits and handicaps, for more sophistication also meant more complexity in maintenance, coupled with a need to preheat the engine before starting to ensure effective lubrication. Less sophistication obviated the need for preheating, but brought some inherent design shortcomings. The two designs even had contrasting versions of hydraulic drive – the hydrodynamic Voith and the hydromechanical Mekydro. Irrespective of

any comparisons between diesel-electric and diesel-hydraulic transmission, here the stage was set for an assessment of a range of other philosophies and practices; for example, NBL chose an electric motor radiator fan drive, but Swindon preferred a hydrostatic one.

The Pilot Scheme
Type 4 diesel-electrics

Turning now to the Type 4 diesel-electric designs within the Pilot Scheme, it was not surprising that one came from English Electric and had many similarities to No 10203, the Southern Region prototype. A strength underframe supported the superstructure and equipment. The overall length was 69ft 6in and the weight 133 tons — 1 ton more than No D10203. The same design of bogie as used on the latter was selected, with a leading unpowered axle and three powered axles; the driving wheel diameter was 3ft 9in. Naturally, the choice for the powertrain mirrored that of No D10203, with the 16SVT Mk II engine of 2,000hp at

No D812 *The Royal Naval Reserve 1859-1959* was the last example to be built without illuminated route-indicator boxes, equipped in instead with a rather ugly metal frame on the nose end to carry train numbers. It is seen passing Slough with a down fitted freight on 27 May 1963, at which time the station's track layout was being 'rationalised'. *P. J. Lynch*

Above: Gerald Fiennes had been instrumental in securing the first batch of BR Standard Class 7 steam locomotives for the Great Eastern, and history repeated itself when the first English Electric Type 4s emerged from Vulcan Foundry. No D209 awaits departure from Norwich for Liverpool Street on 1 July 1961, while Brush Type 2 No D5567 prepares to take an excursion to Wembley Hill. *Author's collection*

Below: The 'D200' class had a long association with the West Coast main line, spanning more than 25 years. Here No D267 calls at Northampton station, as yet unrebuilt, on 3 April 1961 at the head of the 8.40am from Carlisle (9.25am from Windermere) to Euston. *Michael Mensing*

850rpm and an English Electric 822/4C 10-pole main generator rated at 1,313kW, 1,800A, 730V at 850rpm. The six traction motors were the six-pole English Electric 526/5D. The radiator fan was driven mechanically from the engine. The first 10, Nos D200-9, were built as part of the Pilot Scheme, though repeat orders eventually multiplied the class to 200.

Politically, it was inevitable that the BTC should make use of its own railway workshops for diesel-locomotive construction, and so the other Pilot Scheme Type 4 was a design produced by Derby Works. It has been said that the LMR's CM&EE, J. F. Harrison (who succeeded R. C. Bond as British Railways CME in 1958 from the post of LMR CM&EE, when the latter became the BTC's Technical Adviser), favoured the Sulzer LDA28 diesel for locomotives. He envisaged the region's main-line locomotive requirements' being met by two classes, one with a 12-cylinder and the other with a six-cylinder version.

Derby produced a 67ft 11in locomotive, again with an official weight of 133 tons, but the rumour was that the true weight was around 140 tons. Again, the 1Co bogie was used, with a 3ft 9in-diameter driving wheel. The Sulzer 12LDA28 engine's output of 2,300hp at 750rpm in 'A' form was increased to 2,500hp at 750rpm in the 'B' version, which was fitted in the subsequent batches. Coupled to this was a Crompton Parkinson CG426A1 main generator, continuously rated at 1,546/1,531kW, 960/580V, 1,610/2,640A at 1,080rpm. Six CP C171B1 traction motors were mounted traditionally on the driving axles. As with the 'D600s', the radiator fan was driven by an electric motor.

Numbered from D1, the first batch comprised 10 machines. Subsequently the class was multiplied to a total of 193, though the last 56 had Brush electrical machines — the BT TG 160-60 main generator and BT TM73-68 traction motors — substituting for the Crompton Parkinson equipment, and a hydrostatic radiator fan drive replacing the electric fan motor.

The 'overweight' nature of the first two Type 4 designs of diesel-electric that were sanctioned within the Pilot Scheme have often been a vexed issue. Harrison referred to it, in his Presidential address to the Institution

One of the first batch of BR-built Type 4 'Peaks', No D5 *Cross Fell*, approaches Lenton South Junction, Nottingham, with an eastbound freight on 29 April 1966.
J. S. Hancock

of Locomotive Engineers on 26 September 1962, in the following terms:

> From the design point of view great changes have already taken place. When the products of the original design of Type 4 mainline diesel locomotives made their appearance as 1Co-Co1 locomotives, BR was criticised on the grounds that the designs gave a very poor power:weight ratio compared with other designs from European countries. What was not known by the critics at that time was the reasoning behind this particular wheel arrangement. It arose as a consequence of a need to reduce the ratio of axle weight (in tons) to wheel diameter (in feet), or P/D, to a figure not exceeding 4.5.
>
> This ratio was fixed by the Chief Civil Engineer as a wise move to control excessive rail breakage, as such a condition was thought at that time to be one of the main contributory causes of fractured rails. Since 1957 much thought has been given to this problem, and loco designers have also helped in reducing overall weight by the increase of power to weight of the diesel engine and transmissions,

so that the present standard Type 4 mainline loco is being built as a Co-Co of 114 tons compared with the 136 tons of the original 1Co-Co1 giving a hp:weight ratio of 24 compared with 17 and much improved route availability, as the Co-Co is able to negotiate 10-chain vertical curves compared with a minimum of 17-chain vertical curves for the 1Co-Co1 — a matter of some great importance where marshalling yards have no engine escape road. It is interesting to note that the new Krauss-Maffei 4,000hp diesel-hydraulic locos for the US have a hp:weight ratio of 27, without heating boiler and water for same.

The foregoing prompts certain questions. Why did the British Railways CCE impose a much lower limit of 4.5 than his European and American counterparts? What was the basis for his decision? Why was Swindon allowed to exceed this limit with the 'D800' class? At the time that the decisions on the Pilot Scheme designs were taken, J. C. L. Train was the BTC Technical Officer, and among other roles he chaired the Technical Committee. He was therefore superior to Bond, the British Railways CME, but unlike Bond he was a civil engineer. Did politics play a part in preventing any challenge to the British Railways CCE's arbitrary selection of the 4.5 ratio?

Competing Type 3s and Type 2s

The introduction of higher-powered diesel-hydraulic locomotives stalled in the mid-1950s for want of a transmission that was capable of handling more than 1,000hp. *Diesel Railway Traction* for August 1958 covered Maybach's announcement that it had produced the Mekydro K184 model, capable of taking an input of 1,800hp. Up to this point, neither Mekydro nor Voith had in production a transmission capable of taking an input above 1,000hp, and this was limiting the development of higher-powered locomotives. Voith followed quickly with a new version of its L216 torque-converter and a high-input

Above: Later 'Peaks' had an engine rating of 2,500hp and route-indicator boxes on either side of the nose-end gangway doors. On 18 June 1967 No D73 hurries a Sheffield–St Pancras express through Kibworth. *J. H. Cooper-Smith*

Left: No D131 exemplifies the later version of the class the with four-character indicator box. The location is Dove Holes Tunnel, in the Peak District, and the train is the 10.25am Manchester Central–St Pancras, photographed on 17 July 1964. *John Clarke*

Right: From No D138 Brush electrical equipment was substituted for Crompton Parkinson machinery. This is No D169, seen passing Beeston with the up 'Yorkshire Pullman'. *Ian Allan Library*

Below: The Vulcan Foundry's official view of No D6713 when brand-new. Note the plain bodyside, without any lining, and the indicator boxes on either side of the gangway doors. From No D6819 these latter with dispensed with, allowing a neater arrangement with a single four-character box placed centrally. *Ian Allan Library*

model, the L218, which could be used in applications above 1,000hp.

These developments were opportune, because in 1958 British Railways invited tenders for 420 diesel locomotives as part of its 1959-61 Building & Condemnation Programme. Within this total were requests from the ER, NER and WR for 30, 12 and 45 Type 3s respectively. Several builders submitted tenders, which included diesel-hydraulic transmissions for the WR examples. Although the Birmingham Railway Carriage & Wagon Co had submitted the lowest tender for the diesel-electric locomotives, based on a design similar to that already ordered for the Southern Region, BR opted instead to order from English Electric, mainly owing to the large order placed concurrently

for Sulzer/Crompton Parkinson powertrain equipment for the Derby Type 4. The date of the decision was 27 January 1959.

The mechanical portions were a scaled-down No D200, with an overall length of 61ft 6in, but the lower overall weight of 105 tons 13cwt permitted the use of a Co-pattern bogie of a new design. The English Electric Type 3 used a charge-cooled version of the SVT engine that had been in rail service from No 10000 through to the 'D200s'. In its 12-cylinder 12CSVT form for British Railways service it developed 1,750hp at 850rpm. The main generator was the 10-pole English Electric 822/10G, rated at 1,107kW, 1,800A, 615V at 850rpm, and the six English Electric 538/A traction motors were mounted traditionally, one per axle. Numbered from No D6700, the class was eventually multiplied to 309 examples.

As to the diesel-hydraulics for the Western Region, English Electric tried to persuade the BTC to order diesel-electric instead! The minutes of a meeting, held on 4 May 1959 at Paddington and involving the Western Region's Operating, CM&EE and Running & Maintenance departments gives an insight into this design. Discussing the problem of the brake force of the 'D800' class when used on Class E and unbraked freights, the Operating

Above: As with the English Electric Type 4s, the first batch of 'D6700s' went to Stratford for use in East Anglia. On 8 June 1962 No D6716 had to be turned out on a Type 4 duty, the 1.30pm Liverpool Street–Norwich, being seen here leaving Chelmsford. *Michael Mensing*

Above: The 'Hymeks' originally had the horns neatly hidden away at buffer height. No D7000 is seen when new, at Marylebone on 12 May 1961, on the occasion of an Institution of Locomotive Engineers meeting. *Ian Allan Library*

Above: No D7019, by contrast, has roof-mounted horns. It is seen here at Stoke Gifford Yard with the 13.05 from Bath on 19 August 1967. *G. R. Hounsell*

Above: When placing its first orders in 1959 the Western Region envisaged a fleet of several hundred of its Standard Type 3, the 'D7000'. New 'Hymeks' undertook a proving run from Ashbury's carriage sidings, near Beyer Peacock's Gorton Works, via the Peak District, to Derby. No D7041 prepares for its return journey on 27 June 1962. *Alec Swain / Transport Treasury*

Below: Comparison of rival Type 3s at Cardiff General in the mid-1960s, the old-style nose end of English Electric Type 3 No D6842 (right) contrasting with the styling handiwork of E. G. M. Wilkes's 'D7000' design. The former is on a freight, while the 'Hymek' is on passenger duty. *Alec Swain / Transport Treasury*

Department referred to the view it had expressed in early 1958 that the proposed Type 3 should have a C-C wheel arrangement, which would provide greater locomotive braking effort. Its argument had been resisted by the CM&EE on cost grounds and supported by the General Manager; hence the new Type 3 would have a B-B wheel arrangement.

A submission to the Works Committee dated 21 April 1959 came down in favour of diesel-hydraulic on both price and delivery date. Beyer Peacock's Hymek consortium submitted the lowest price, and the submission noted that there was some commonality in equipment with the 'D800s'.

The Hymek diesel-hydraulic was of orthodox (not monocoque) construction, and was 51ft 8½in long. For the desired route availability, a maximum axle load of 18½ tons was stipulated. The overall weight was 75 tons 8cwt and thus slightly over the limit, but the locomotive could still be mounted on two-axle bogies. Maybach had been developing both its engine range to include intercooling and its Mekydro transmission to accept an input of 1,800hp. A 16-cylinder MD870 engine, rated officially at 1,700hp at 1,500rpm, was matched to a K184 transmission, which drove all four axles. Two additional batches were ordered, bringing the class total to 101. Numbers from No D7000 were assigned. It is worth noting the parallel development in Germany of the 'V160' class described in Chapter 6.

Two other classes must be mentioned, the NBL Type 2s. These were virtually identical, except that one had hydraulic and the other electric transmission. The former comprised six locomotives and were described in Chapter 7, being part of the initial order on NBL for 11 machines placed in March 1955. The powertrain was one set of the MAN/Voith equipment that was fitted in the 'D600s', but here it drove all four axles. As part of the Pilot Scheme, and with the stated objective of giving a direct comparison between the two forms of transmission, NBL received an order for 10 units with the MAN L12V18/21A engine but with GEC electrical machines. In both applications, the engine was set to develop 1,000hp, though at

1,500rpm for the electric drive and 1,445rpm for the hydraulic. By way of contrast, the following dimensions are salient:

	Diesel-electric	Diesel-hydraulic
Overall length	51ft 6in	46ft 8½in
Weight	72 tons 10cwt	67 tons 16cwt

The diesel-electric version became the 'D6100' class, while the diesel-hydraulics were numbered from No D6300. Further orders came NBL's way for both types, each class eventually totalling 58. By now, MAN had produced the 'B' version of its engine, and the rating became 1,100hp at 1,530rpm. Of course, the concept of a Type 2 machine was a natural choice, and reflected the pioneering examples of the DB's 'V100' class, though the latter had a single cab (see Chapter 6).

Compare and contrast

The foregoing sets out the key technical features of the designs ordered in the Pilot Scheme and the first wave of mass dieselisation. It is now appropriate to review whether the claims by the proponents of diesel-hydraulic transmission proved justified; these were that the resultant locomotive was lighter in weight and cheaper to build, and

Having crossed the Forth Bridge NBL Type 2 diesel-electric No D6142 approaches Dalmeny with a southbound goods on 14 July 1960. Just visible below the rear driver's-side window is the single-line tablet-exchange equipment that marks out the locomotive as being allocated to Aberdeen Kittybrewster. Shortly after this photograph was taken use of the class south of Dundee on the route to Edinburgh ceased for several years, because the class was moved to other duties. *C. P. Boocock*

Above: On 13 May 1961, when this picture was taken, the running of a combined service from Glasgow Buchanan Street and Edinburgh Princes Street to Oban had not long to go. NBL Type 2s Nos D6108 and D6135 are seen after arrival at Oban. *Michael Mensing*

Right: Later builds of the 'D6300' diesel-hydraulics had route-indicator boxes. In charge of a short mixed goods, No D6313 passes through Bedminster on 13 January 1968. *P. J. Fowler*

The start of the Hemyock branch from Tiverton Junction is the location for this view of No D6330 in charge of the 13.45 milk empties from Exeter on 15 July 1970. *John M. Boyes*

offered a lower continuous rating than comparable diesel-electric traction.

There is a problem in determining the actual cost of a locomotive, in that manufacturers sometimes came back to the BTC with a price increase for this reason or that, and in the 1960s English Electric put forward a retrospective quantity-discount arrangement. Even more difficult was getting at the true cost of locomotives built in railway workshops, and this was to prove a highly controversial issue for the 'D1000' class, to be described later. The following table shows some comparative statistics.

Multiplying the continuous tractive effort by the speed and dividing by the constant 375

Comparative build costs and performance

Class	Cost each (£)	Weight (tons)	Continuous rating (lb)	Speed (mph)	Power at rail (hp)	Transmission efficiency (%)
D11[a]	127,000	136	30,000	25.0	2,000	80
D200	100,000[b]	133	30,900	18.8	1,549	77.45
D600	86,000[c]	117	39,600	12.6	1,331	66.55
D800						
Swindon	100,000[d]	78	46,700	10.7	1,333	60.6
NBL	115,167	80	37,000	14.0	1,381	62.8
D6700	84,000[e]	106	35,000	13.6	1,269	72.5
D7000	79,730[f]	75	33,950	12.5	1,132	66.6
D6100[g]	62,400	72.5	30,000	10.2	816	74.1
D6300[g]	53,000	65	30,000	8.0	640	58.2

a 2,500hp version with Crompton Parkinson electrical machines. Nos D1-10 cost £129,371.
b Typical cost. Nos D200-9 cost £106,000, the next batch £98,500; costs rose for later orders.
c Tender at 1953 prices, increased later to reflect 1956/7 prices.
d 2,200hp production versions (but Swindon cost estimated only).
e Revised price for Nos D6700-41; the next batch cost £88,000.
f Initial price for 45; the next batch cost £81,000, the final six £77,696.
g Cost for Pilot Scheme order; other details for production series.
   The 'D6100' production series cost £66,785, the 'D6300' production series £63,175.

gives the rail horsepower. Although by no means necessarily the peak rhp value, this gives an approximation of the transmission efficiency, in other words, how much of the engine power is available for traction after losses in the powertrain and in powering auxiliaries.

Even allowing for costs' varying down the years and being dependent on the quantity being ordered (more = lower unit price), the table establishes irrefutably that:

1. Hydraulic locomotives were lighter, even when traditional construction was adopted
2. Hydraulic locomotives cost less, but locomotives built in railway shops cost more than those built by contractors, where actual figures are available
3. For locomotives of equivalent power designed for mixed-traffic work and with the same top speed, the continuous rating was at a lower speed with diesel-hydraulic transmission

Later Type 4s

The technological advance of charge-air cooling (intercooling) a diesel engine in order to increase its power began to be felt in rail traction during the last couple of years of the 1950s. Mention of this has already been made in connection with the new engines produced by English Electric, Maybach and Sulzer for the units fitted in the 'D6700s' and 'D7000s' and in the 'D1s' from No D11. Both English Electric and Sulzer made further progress in this area, though British Railways decided to adopt 2,750hp as its standard for future Type 4 designs.

The Western Region's new Type 4

What became the 'D1000' class can claim to be the most controversial diesel type ever built, at least from an enthusiast's perspective. Much has been written about this highly popular design, by no means all of which bears scrutiny against the official record.

The earliest date tracked down in the official records for the 'D1000' class was during a BTC meeting on 23 May 1957, when K. W. C. Grand, the Western Region's General Manager, mentioned his interest in acquiring a 3,000hp locomotive to work heavy coal trains. Preliminary design work was put in hand, and the subject was discussed at the Western Region Area Board meeting on 18 June 1958. It was reported that agreement had been reached with the BTC CME (by then J. F. Harrison) for a 2,700hp locomotive to handle the Western Region's principal services. The increase in horsepower was based on experience gained with the 2,200hp 'D800s' and was justified by the desire to improve services and ensure a high standard of punctuality. That this was only an agreement in principle can be seen by ratification of the decision at a meeting on 9 February 1959 between the chairman of the Western Region Area Board, the BTC's Technical Officer, and his Technical Adviser (now R. C. Bond), both of whom were senior to the BTC CME.

Having decided on a new Type 4 design, not one of 3,000hp, for mixed-traffic duties, along with other regions, the Western Region submitted proposals for its next phase of dieselisation to the BTC in November 1958 for outline approval. The plans covered a combined Area 1 (west of Newton Abbot) and Area 2 (Bristol), because the Region believed that better economy would be gained by virtue of the amount of through working from London. With the exception of the 22 'Deltics' ordered for the East Coast main line nothing more powerful than a Type 4 had yet been sanctioned, and the BTC approved in principle the purchase of 79 locomotives of that power. In the event, the lead time between the ending of construction of the 'D800s' at Swindon and the start on the 'D1000s' brought an application for five of the new Type 4s to be built instead, as an extension of the former class, in order to ensure continuity in the Works; these became Nos D866-70.

At the Works Committee meeting on 1 January 1959 it was reported that the Western Region had received quotations for the power equipment for the 2,700hp Type 4. Recommendation of the equipment to be ordered was to be made after 'certain technical questions had been settled'.

It was to be June 1959 before the new Western Region General Manager, Roy Hammond, put a firm proposal to the Works Committee for the Western Region's final requirements for Areas 1 and 2. These included 74 diesel-hydraulics of 2,700hp. This submission is highly illuminating and is paraphrased below. First, however, it should be noted that Hammond envisaged the use of diesel-hydraulic traction for Area 3 (Wales) but diesel-electric for Area 4 (London to Birmingham and the North). This was because of the inter-regional operation of the latter.

Hammond was content with a locomotive of 2,700hp, which, he said, could be stepped up to 3,000hp for further traffic developments or the fitting of electric train heating (ETH), if required 'at minimal cost'. A re-geared 3,000hp unit, based on the new Type 4, could be developed for the heaviest mineral traffic in South Wales, and would then fit into the Western Region's planning and remove the need for a further new type, previously envisaged as a 3,300hp. The new Type 4 was to be a straightforward development of the 'D800' class, with a high degree of standardisation of general construction and components, including power equipment.

> Questions of rail stress and adhesion [wrote Hammond], which have arisen with the smaller B-B type [the 'D800s'], would probably have necessitated redesign as a C-C (like the proposed new Type 4). The cost of such a [redesigned] locomotive, at £110,000, would not be significantly less than that of the proposed 2,700hp unit at between £115,000 and £120,000.

What is startling from the above is the note of dissatisfaction with the performance of the 'D800s' only a couple of months before G. E. Scholes read his paper to the Institution of Locomotive Engineers, in which he was complimentary about the type. From the foregoing it is abundantly clear that, *at that time*, the Western Region remained content with a 2,700hp mixed-traffic machine and envisaged a requirement for 3,000hp only in special circumstances.

The 'D1000s' had a wheel diameter of 45in — six inches more than that of the 'D800s'. A possible clue to this change can be found in a paper presented in 1962 by S. O. Ell, the head of the Swindon Outside Testing Section. He expounded that, unlike their steam counterparts, diesel locomotives had to be general-purpose, mixed-traffic machines, equally at home on fast passenger and slow heavy-freight services. A contemporary problem, to which at that time no end was in sight, was the ongoing non-availability of continuously braked wagons.

The efficiency of braking falls as the intensity of brake-block pressure increases, and the heat generated is dissipated less well from small wheels than from the large wheels of steam locomotives. A B-B locomotive (like the 'D800s'), especially if it has small wheels, is more prone to suffer from brake fade and tyre trouble than a C-C locomotive with the largest wheels it is possible to fit.

At the time of the Modernisation Plan's promulgation in 1955, it was envisaged that the policy of fitting vacuum brakes to all freight stock would be completed quickly. It was only this understanding that justified the employment on freight workings of a B-B locomotive with 39½in-diameter wheels. Clearly, three years on, and with the universal fully fitted freight still some way off, the Western Region had to rethink the requirements for locomotive braking, and this was probably the reason for the increase in wheel diameter. The change also brought the 'D1000' design into line with the prevailing BTC thinking on the P/D ratio of locomotive weight to wheel diameter.

By 1959 Krauss-Maffei in Germany had rebuilt its C-C prototype, No ML3000, with two Maybach MD655 engines rated at 3,000hp. As noted in Chapter 6, this locomotive had first emerged in 1957, fitted with MD650 engines rated at 2,200hp, and its mechanical parts provided the design inspiration for the 'D1000s'. This is clear from the oblique reference to this prototype in Hammond's submission.

The foregoing, based entirely on official records, explains why the new design for the Western Region was of a 2,700hp machine mounted on three-axle bogies, based on the ML3000 mechanical parts and with a wheel diameter in keeping with previous British Railways practice. It is interesting to refer back to Chapter 6 and DB's parallel approach to the production of a locomotive of similar power, the 'V200'[1]. Krauss-Maffei used the B-B mechanical parts of the 'V200' but, without the same loading-gauge and locomotive-brake-force constraints that applied on the Western Region, was able to accommodate the desired higher-output powertrain in the 'V200' body.

Moving on to some key features of the design, the choice of engine for the 'D1000' class was interesting. At the time it was made, there would have been only limited British experience with the Maybach and MAN engines fitted in the 'D800s'. Maybach had applied intercooling to its MD650, and the new engine was coded the MD655. This new engine passed its UIC testing at a rating of 1,500hp at 1,500rpm, but for application in the 'D1000s' the official rating chosen was 1,350hp, though some sources report that Swindon set the engines at 1,380hp. In truth, 30hp would be the tolerance range for a nominal rating of this power, and Swindon lacked an engine test plant to load-test overhauled engines until 1967, so getting a precise rating before then would have been difficult. Jeremy Clarke, a Western Region locomotive engineer from 1963 to 1989, comments that Swindon set engine horsepower within a specified tolerance band and did not spend too much time tuning the engine to get a particular horsepower. The settings soon seemed to change for one reason or another once an engine went into service.

At this time Swindon was building the 'D800s' with the Mekydro K104 transmission, and it would have been natural to select the 1,800hp K184 for the 'D1000s'. In his 1959 paper on the 'D800' class Scholes set out several perceived advantages of the Mekydro arrangement. No official source has explained why the choice for the 'D1000s' was not the Mekydro, but at a meeting of the Institution of Mechanical Engineers' Railway Branch at Swindon in February 2010 the consensus among former Western Region engineers was that the K184 could not be delivered in time. Although J. Stone & Co was building K184 transmissions at the time, they were for the 'D7000s', and Stone was therefore unable or unwilling to double its production output to fulfil an order for the 'D1000s'. Tantalisingly, as described earlier, the minutes of the Works Committee meeting on 1 January 1959 concerning the choice of transmission refer to the decision's being delayed until 'certain technical questions had been settled'. These may, however, have related to the location of the L630 output shaft. All the other L630 and L830 converters built by Voith were 'U' variants, with the output shaft located higher than on the 'V' variant, in which it was set low down, and the latter was a model made specifically for the 'D1000s', to address the design parameters for the locomotive.

The next option was to see what Voith could offer. Before describing the transmission it is necessary to make a diversion into the evolution of the Voith torque-converter. By 1958 the company had in production the L216 unit of 1,300hp input, which was being used in the latest 'V100s' of similar power, and the L218, which was being fitted in the 'V160s' of 1,900hp. These transmissions had two torque-converter circuits and a fluid coupling, and therefore needed a two-range gear drive to provide a suitable tractive effort/speed curve across the full speed range up to 100mph, as in the 'V320'. Probably prompted by Krauss-Maffei, Voith recognised that, while this was acceptable to German Federal Railways, export markets would expect a transmission that provided full rating across the whole speed band without the need for low- and high-speed gear ranges. As a result, in 1959 Voith produced two new three-stage torque-converters, Krauss-Maffei being the first client.

The Voith L630r was of 1,300hp input (Voith size 6, with three torque-converters and no fluid coupling) while the L830r was of 1,800hp input (size 8). These were developed to provide a very high starting tractive effort. The L630r offered a fine power control at very low speed, which British Railways opted to take, and a hydrodynamic braking facility, which it did not.

There is a prevailing view among enthusiasts that the L630 was not the intended transmission but that Voith had offered to produce a new model for the 'D1000s'. This question has been raised with Wolfgang Paetzold, who retired in 1995 as Voith's Chief Engineering Manager for rail, was then commissioned by the company to write the complete history of Voith Turbo, and worked on the 'D1000' project in Britain. Here is his reply, including his response concerning the L630rV:

The starting torque-converter was a new development with two turbines and a very high standstill torque. This was essential, since all three torque-converters were hydraulically staggered. Voith was very proud of this new type of torque-converter. Instead of the fluid coupling of the L216rs for the Deutsche Bundesbahn, another two-stage torque-converter for the medium speed range was developed. Lastly, the third torque-converter was employed as a torque-converter for high speeds.

The rumour about an improved torque-converter for the 'D1000' I cannot confirm; I never heard of such an intention. The three torque-converter design was used for all transmissions size 6 and 8, *i.e.* also for the North American L830rU transmissions (used by Krauss-Maffei and Alco). For standardisation reasons, I feel, it was never seriously considered.

A separate paper written by Herr Paetzold gives further insight into this important period of development, and has implications for the 'D1000' troubles that will be covered in Chapter 10. After 1953, of great importance was Voith's introduction of the torsional flexible coupling and the systematic torsional analysis of the engine-transmission system, including auxiliaries, and the secondary mass system of the locomotive or railcar. The development of the L630 and L830 torque-converters was highly significant. This was the first time that three hydraulically staggered torque-converters had been used, placed on a common impeller quill shaft and a common turbine shaft. It allowed the separation of the hydraulic and mechanical sections, and minimised the number of gears needed.

Continuing with the D1000 project, a major problem was the need to move the transmission sets from under the cab to the centre of the locomotive. It arose because the British loading-gauge is lower than on the Continent, and also because of the decision to make the bogie wheels 6in larger than those of the 'D800s'. Consequently, the transmission had to be modified to relocate the output shaft. Furthermore, the intermediate transmission and bogie had to be turned through 180° from the position used in a build of 2,700hp locomotives for Turkey by Krauss-Maffei in June 1961, which also had the Voith L630r transmission but with the output shaft located differently, bringing the designation L630rU, as against L630rV for the model produced by Voith for British Railways. Swindon used the bogies designed by Krauss-Maffei for ML3000, which were a three-axle version of those used for the 'D800s'. Overall weight was 108 tons.

British Railways invited tenders from NBL and the Hymek consortium, as well as its own shops at Crewe and Swindon. A memorandum of 19 August 1959 from the BR Chief Contracts Officer and the CME evaluated the bids. The original intention had been to involve the private sector in construction of the major part of the order. By continuing to build the standard British Railways 350hp shunter at Horwich after 1960, this would have allowed capacity at Crewe for building the new Type 4. The British Railways works quoted £115,000 per locomotive, NBL £123,900 and Hymek £136,000, which figures should be remembered in the light of the actual build costs. All the tenders were on the same footing, using the MD655 engine and the L306rV transmission. (Voith changed its nomenclature shortly afterwards, so that the transmission became the L630rV.)

Interesting remarks were made about the contractors. Concerning NBL, it was said that deliveries to date had been 'far from satisfactory' and that 'performance does not inspire confidence'. As to Hymek, this was 'a powerful consortium', but it had only just secured its first order, and the possibility of teething troubles could not be ruled out.

The memorandum therefore recommended 74 Type 4s for Western Region Areas 1 and 2, to be built in British Railways shops, and the BTC gave approval on 27 August for building locomotives at Crewe and Swindon at an estimated total cost of £8,550,000. On 2 November 1959 the Chief Contracts Officer recommended to the Supply Committee the placing of orders with Bristol Siddeley for 74 sets of engines and (initially) 25 torque-converters from NBL. Manufacture of the torque-converters was expected to be split between NBL and Voith in order to meet British Railways' build requirements. J. Stone & Co was to supply the transmission accessories and Brush the control gear. Bristol Siddeley was invited to act as main contractor for the powertrain, but when British Railways realised that it would save money if Swindon fulfilled this role, the decision was (as always) to take the cheaper option; this was to prove an expensive mistake, as will be seen in Chapter 10.

The story of the external styling is interesting. Once again, the Design Research Unit was contracted by the BTC to handle it. The Western Region General Manager wanted to retain the 'D800' appearance, which had not proved universally popular. The alternative, which was finally adopted, was sold to the General Manager by a persuasive

argument that surely he would prefer something distinctively Western Region rather than just a copy of a German design.

The initial order on Voith via NBL was for 60 transmissions, with a maximum weight not to exceed 3½ tons, which was achieved within a tolerance of 3%. A larger torque-converter could not therefore have been accommodated. Delivery dates were, however, missed, and the first two did not arrive until February 1961, but some revisions were needed and took until 31 July to implement, delaying completion of No D1000 until the end of 1961. The first 60 transmissions were manufactured by Voith in Heidenheim, and the remaining 103 in Glasgow.

How much did the 'D1000' class cost? Being an internal project, there was no tender figure. Estimates fluctuated up and down from £135,000 to £115,000 each. Matters came to a head in 1962 when Bond, the BTC Technical Adviser, picked up with great concern on figures from the WR and LMR for 1961, which were £131,230 and £119,104 respectively. It was acknowledged that Swindon costs were higher because piece

rates there had always been high, while there was also greater competition in the retention of skilled staff, who could easily find employment elsewhere. Both figures were still estimates and were to be ignored! There was none of the commercial rigour here that applied to a private contractor; just look at the comparative figures above for the later 'Peaks' (No D11 onwards) and the 'D200s'.

At the time of Hammond's submission of June 1959 he stated that 30 locomotives would be built at Swindon, with the rest put out to contractors. In the event, Crewe Works undertook the building of 44, and Swindon 30.

The Standard British Railways Type 4 diesel-electric

The final design to be dealt with here is what ended up as British Railways' standard Type 4. Its development started internally in 1959, specifying a Co-Co wheel arrangement and a gross power of at least 2,500hp. This was paralleled by an invitation from the BTC for manufacturers to produce designs of their own. This proved to be a waste of time and money for the three companies that built

Comparison of Swindon-designed Type 4s — 'Western' No D1047 *Western Lord* (left) and 'Warship' No D870 *Zulu*, photographed at Swindon Works on 15 May 1963. *Ian Allan Library*

prototype locomotives, namely the Birmingham Railway Carriage & Wagon Co (No D0260 *Lion*), Brush (No D0280 *Falcon*) and English Electric (No DP2). Why a waste? Because British Railways (and reportedly J. F. Harrison, the Central Staff CME) had decided views on what it did and did not want.

No D0260 had Sulzer's 12-cylinder LDA28 diesel in the latest 'C' version, rated at 2,750hp at 800rpm, and AEI electrical machines. The overall weight was 114 tons, and the locomotive was handed to British Railways during May 1962.

No D0280 had two Maybach 12-cylinder MD655 engines, each rated at 1,400hp at 1,500rpm and manufactured by Bristol Siddeley, which was part of the same group of companies as Brush. Unsurprisingly, Brush electrical machines were used. Completed by September 1961, the locomotive was handed over to British Railways the following month.

During a visit to Brush while construction was in hand, Harrison is believed to have expressed no interest in the prototype, because of its high-speed engines. Of note was the use of monocoque construction techniques, which contributed to an overall weight of just 115 tons.

For No DP2 English Electric, in order to produce a prototype quickly, used a set of mechanical parts that were very similar to those being constructed for the production-series 'Deltics'. The company's CSVT Mk 2 engine, being fitted in 12-cylinder form in the 'D6700s' but here with 16 cylinders, was now rated at 2,700hp at 850rpm. Again, naturally, English Electric used electrical machines of its own manufacture, and the overall weight was a creditable 105 tons, though how English Electric produced a machine with a larger power unit than the 'D6700' class but at a lower weight is a mystery. Again, handover to BR took place in May 1962. The twists and

Another styling contrast, this time at Gloucester Horton Road. 'Western' No D1040 *Western Queen* and 'Warship' No D836 *Powerful* frame an unidentified 'Peak' on 3 March 1970. *N. E. Preedy*

Above: Produced by a consortium comprising BRCW, AEI and Sulzer, No D0260 *Lion* commenced trial running on BR in 1962, being pictured on 23 May at the foot of the Lickey Incline with a 16-coach train of 495 tons. The locomotive was to have a short life, being dismantled as early as 1964 after BRCW ran into financial difficulties. *Sulzer Bros*

Below: By the early 1960s technology had advanced, and higher-powered locomotives could be produced. Brush Electrical Engineering Co Ltd built No D0280 *Falcon*, which had twin Maybach MD655 engines but electric transmission. The prototype is seen north of Essendine with the up 'Sheffield Pullman' on 24 May 1962. *R. Howell*

turns that had led to Brush being given an order for 20 new Type 4s are complex; suffice it to say that the BTC opted for a new design, which would incorporate the Sulzer 12LDA-28C engine of 2,750hp at 800rpm, with Brush electrical equipment. Although the BTC had issued tenders in May 1960 for 100 locomotives, the decision to order 20 from Brush was to absorb the electrical machines already ordered from the company for a batch of 76 'Peaks', which the BTC now wished to reduce to 56. The overall weight for these 20 is often quoted as 117 tons, though the later British Railways design code (474AX) covering Nos D1500-19 referred to 121 tons. As with No D0280, monocoque techniques were used for the mechanical parts.

The cost of the new design for a run of 20 was £113,250. British Railways wanted its own workshops at Crewe to become involved in construction of the new standard Type 4, and

when a further tender was issued in 1962 it submitted a price of £107,259 per locomotive, based on the Brush design, as against £111,250 by Brush for a run of 50. Despite lower tenders from other manufacturers for different designs, the BTC stuck with the Brush product. Eventually, the class, numbered from No D1500, totalled 512, with production shared between Brush and Crewe. Styling was inspired by E. J. Wilkes, of Wilkes & Ashmore, which had been engaged by Brush for No D0280 and by the BTC for the 'D7000s', aswell as the 'D1500s', hence the family resemblance. Whereas all the other production-series classes considered in this chapter had a maximum speed of 90mph, the 'D1500s' were passed to run at 95mph.

The foregoing shows considerable variation in concept and design between locomotives that emerged over a five-year period. Applying intercooling to engines saw

In mechanical terms similar to the later Class 50 design, English Electric prototype DP2 utilised a shortened 'Deltic' bodyshell. Seen near Lancaster with a down express in April 1963, it too would have its career truncated, being withdrawn as a result of serious damage sustained in an accident near York in July 1967. *A. E. R. Cope / Colour-Rail (DE321)*

power per cylinder rise dramatically. The design of electrical machines and hydraulic transmission also progressed to be able to absorb the higher power outputs of the engines. Finally, the monocoque construction methods first seen in the 'V200' class were eventually adopted in Britain, and they kept overall locomotive weights down.

Factor into this mix the background of events on British Railways at the time, such as the unforeseen slow pace of the change to fully braked freight rolling stock, and different patterns of utilisation of the classes, and the result is a complex mix of parameters against which to establish any meaningful comparison. Prolonged running at high power load factors at high speed will always be more demanding than short-duration, low-speed mineral traffic duties.

Nevertheless, by 1962 it had proved possible to construct a 2,700hp diesel-electric (No DP2) that weighed less than a comparable diesel-hydraulic. True, 4,000hp locomotives were shortly to emerge on the Continent, making use of high-speed engines and hydraulic drive, but, with a 19½-ton axle load, their performance could have been replicated with electric transmission too. Crewe Works could build a diesel-electric for less than an equivalent diesel-hydraulic. What had not changed, for mixed-traffic designs, was the disparity between the continuous rating of diesel-electric and diesel-hydraulic drives. The performance of the 'D1000' was 45,200lb at 14½mph, and of the 'D1500' 30,000lb at 27mph, and the latter figure was to cause problems with coal train flows, especially on the Eastern Region.

Brush Type 4 No D1565, brand-new at Crewe Works on 8 March 1964, showing clearly how the buffing loads were transmitted to the solebars.
Ian Allan Library

Left: No D1573 on a trial run from Crewe Works, seen near Wigan in April 1964. *Rail Photoprints*

Below: A contrast in size and styling: BR 'Peak' Type 4 No D89 and Brush Type 4s Nos D1603 and D1713 at Gloucester Horton Road on 13 March 1965. *Rail Photoprints*

9

DMU EVOLUTION TO 1975

Arising from the BTC report of October 1951, in September 1952 the Carriage & Wagon Drawing Office at Derby initiated an investigation into a new design of diesel multiple-unit. It was decided that construction would be in high-duty light alloy, in order to give the power-to-weight ratio necessary for the services envisaged, employing integral body and underframe construction. The ICI Metals Division was invited to co-operate in the design of this body structure. The diesel engines were to be the six-cylinder 125hp Leyland L600 type.

The first scheme was for the West Riding, and required eight two-car sets, with all cars powered, to meet operating requirements over rather difficult terrain. Although the mechanical drive used in the GWR railcars had proved to be reasonably successful, Derby chose the same drive arrangement used in the LMS three-car set of 1938, comprising a Leyland-Lysholm-Smith torque-converter and a Walker Bros final drive. Unfortunately,

by then Leyland had superseded the torque-converter for road-transport applications, and no further development had been carried out on what was now an obsolete piece of equipment. Design began in December 1952, and the trains had to be available within 15 months. The first set ran trials in April 1954 in the Leicester area, and the new service began on 14 June.

The next scheme was for West Cumberland, followed by Lincolnshire. The sets for these areas had the same Leyland diesel as the West Yorkshire sets, but they were now rated at 150hp and fitted with a fluid coupling and mechanical drive through a four-speed epicyclic gearbox, an arrangement that became the standard for the future.

During 1954 the Area Boards put forward major schemes for the replacement of steam by lightweight diesel multiple-units (DMUs). Coincident was the availability of the Leyland engine at the higher output of 150hp, while Rolls-Royce offered its six-cylinder engine at 180hp. The higher power now made it unnecessary to construct all DMUs in the relatively more expensive light alloy.

By the end of 1955 British Railways had on order 1,267 diesel DMU vehicles, both from its own works and from private industry.

The first series of postwar DMUs were built by Derby Works for services in the West Riding of Yorkshire. A Carlisle–Bradford train is pictured at Dent on 30 April 1960.
J. S. Hancock

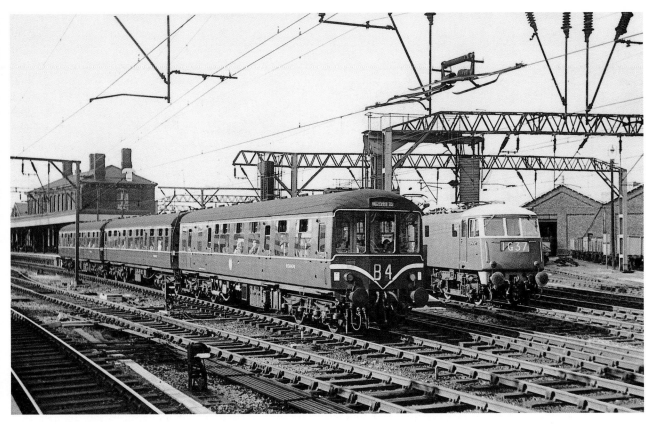

A typical DMU, with 150hp BUT engines and four-speed gearbox. This three-car BRCW unit (later Class 104) is covering a Manchester London Road (now Piccadilly)–Macclesfield service on 5 July 1961, in the days before full electrification at Stockport.
Ian Allan Library

These were additional to those already placed in service in the West Riding, Cumbria, Lincolnshire and County Durham. All of the new orders had a powertrain mounted under the vehicle floor, comprising the six-cylinder British United Traction (BUT) engine of 150hp, connected via a fluid coupling to a four-speed gearbox. BUT was a joint-venture company set up by Leyland and AEC. At the same time a couple of LMR diesel units were rebuilt with Paxman 450hp flat engines below the car floor.

As with the policy of high-volume main-line diesel-locomotive production, the net for DMU builders was cast wide. Some specialism also crept in, with engines other than the BUT 150hp type, to fulfil particular requirements. Several types also received a hydraulic drive in place of the standard mechanical arrangement; this was a Lysholm-Smith type of torque-converter that had been developed further by the Twin Disc Clutch Co of the USA. It had the usual centrifugal pump or impeller, centripetal motor or turbine and the reaction member. The turbine had three sets of vanes,

each receiving fluid in turn, with the reaction or guide vanes attached to the converter casing. The source of the fluid for the torque-converter was the main diesel fuel tank. Rolls-Royce took out a licence in 1956 with a view to producing transmissions of 60-600hp. This transmission was coupled to the Rolls-Royce 238hp engine for British Railways applications at the time, and was installed in the Derby-built sets for the Lea Valley operating out of Liverpool Street, and also to some Cravens-built sets for the LMR, together with the sets described below.

By way of example, during 1959 and 1960 30 four-car DMUs configured for suburban use were built at Derby Works for services from St Pancras to Bedford and Luton. The St Pancras units comprised two outer powered vehicles and two inner trailers, giving a gross weight of 136 tons. Each power car had two 238hp Rolls-Royce C8N engines of 1,800rpm, amounting to 950hp for the set. Attached to each engine was a Rolls-Royce Twin Disc DFR.10000 three-stage torque-converter with the option of direct drive.

Two designs of DMU from Derby Works were equipped with hydraulic transmission, both of them for suburban services. One (later Class 125) was built for services out of Liverpool Street along the Lea Valley; the other (Class 127) worked the Midland-line diagrams out of St Pancras. Here, on 19 August 1976, the 17.17 Moorgate–St Albans leaves Farringdon. *Kevin Lane*

A paper delivered on 6 March 1962 by A. E. Robson, Works Manager at Derby, to the Institution of Locomotive Engineers describes performance issues to that date. The BUT engines were generally trouble-free; the 238hp Rolls-Royce type gave some initial problems, but these were soon rectified. Referring to the same engines fitted to the Cravens sets, which operated in the Manchester area, Robson noted the need for a campaign change of these units, but gave no details. The epicyclic gearbox was also generally trouble-free. The converter portion of the torque-converter was trouble-free, but seizures of the clutch plates engaging direct drive were rather frequent, until an improvement was made in the distribution of lubricant over the clutch faces. Experience with the St Pancras units, fitted with the Twin Disc design of drive, was less happy. They were deployed on a gruelling rail service requiring rapid acceleration from frequent stops. The main problem area — the final drive to the axles — was eventually resolved.

Subsequently the eight-cylinder Rolls-Royce engines suffered from fires; they appeared to be due to the diesel fuel, which was also used as the converter fluid, being heated above its combustion temperature while it was in the torque-converter. Later, lubricating oil was substituted for diesel fuel as the converter fluid. In 1963 Rolls-Royce won a contract with Portuguese Railways for the supply of 19 powertrain sets, comprising 348hp Rolls-Royce engines and hydraulic transmissions (two per twin set) for DMUs built in Portugal. This equipment survived until the sets were refurbished *c*2002.

Southern Region units

Those who might be regarded as 'anti-GWR' refer to the Western Region's adoption of diesel-hydraulic drive for main-line diesels as typical of its tradition of wanting to be different from other regions, yet no such comment is made about the Southern Region's adoption of diesel-electric propulsion for its DMU fleet.

Adopting this arrangement on the Southern Region made more sense than it would have done on other regions, because it represented the substitution of a diesel engine for the third-rail power supply and because the Southern Region already had an electrical

Left: Swindon built all the DMUs that might be termed (formally or informally) 'Inter-City'. The six-car 'Trans-Pennine' sets (later Class 124) could lay claim to this title because they were built for the Liverpool Lime Street–Hull route. They were delayed pending availability of 230hp Albion engines, matched to the standard mechanical gearbox, the total power of 1,840hp giving them the highest power-to-weight ratio of any first-generation DMU. The 2pm ex Liverpool accelerates from a stop at Manchester Exchange through neighbouring Victoria before tackling the fearsome Miles Platting Bank on 10 March 1961. *Ian G. Holt*

engineering side set up maintain the electrical machines. Such a set-up would have been too expensive to replicate nationally, in a way that was not necessary with diesel-mechanical units. Nevertheless, E. S. Cox and S. B. Warder both record that the proposals met with strong opposition and won through only due to the tenacity of one BTC officer. It seems that no one else was prepared to give serious consideration to the use of an engine and generator set of 500hp above the floor.

A subsequent upgrading to 600hp was for special application in Hampshire.

In 1954, when all the regions worked up schemes for the introduction of DMUs, the Southern Region had to take urgent steps to meet increasing public pressure for the improvement of services on the line between London and Hastings via Tunbridge Wells.

The choice of engine fell to the four-cylinder English Electric SRKT. This was from the same range of engines installed in the

Left: Another Swindon product but with the standard powertrain was the 'Cross-Country' design of three-car DMU (later Class 120). Being rather heavier than virtually all other DMUs, it had a low power-to-weight ratio. The final variant sported a four-character route indicator box, as seen on this set at Newport, leading a seven-car formation (the final vehicle being a single parcels car) *en route* from Cardiff to Birmingham New Street via Hereford. *P. J. Sharpe*

Right: A six-car Class 201 'Hastings' DEMU forming the 14.30 Charing Cross–Hastings emerges from Polhill Tunnel on 30 May 1973. *J. H. Cooper-Smith*

Right: The so-called 'Hampshire' units were also diesel-electrics. Class 205 set No 1112 passes Rye windmill (nowadays Grade II listed) on an Ashford–Hastings turn on 5 September 1984. *Ian Allan Library*

standard British Railways 350hp shunters, while the identical engine-and-generator set, at the same rating, had been supplied by English Electric to Egypt in 1947 (see Chapter 1). For the 'Hastings' sets the rating was 500hp at 850rpm. An EE824/2b main generator was used to supply power to two standard Southern Region EE507 traction motors. The engine and generator set was mounted in a compartment behind the driver, with passenger accommodation in the remainder of the vehicle. One of these power cars was attached at each end of the six-car set.

The coach-body design followed that of the standard British Railways Mk 1 carriage of 1951, unlike the DMUs produced for the other regions, which had a more modern, lighter, airy style. In consequence (and as would happen again later with the EMU stock built in the 1960s for the Bournemouth-line electrification) the Southern Region was provided with a train that was already out of date, in terms of passenger appeal, by the time it entered service.

The first stage of the 'Hastings' DEMU timetable was introduced on 17 June 1957 using seven six-coach units, the full service, with a total of 23 six-coach units, being implemented with effect from 9 June 1958.

On 18 October 1960 W. J. A. Sykes, the Southern Region's CM&EE, delivered to the Institution of Locomotive Engineers a paper in which he commented on the performance of the 'Hastings' DEMUs. After some teething troubles with the engines, the first one was stripped down at between 7,000 and 8,000 hours. Its condition was found to be satisfactory, and this experience proved to be the case generally. Initial experience with the main generator and traction motors brought a requirement for a change in brush grade, because the original type wore out excessively quickly. Thereafter the electric drive proved trouble-free. The operating and maintenance costs of these units compared favourably with their diesel-mechanical counterparts.

To draw some general conclusions, British Railways' DMU fleet embraced mechanical, hydraulic and electrical power transmission. It is probably fair to say that the diesel-hydraulic units suffered from the design flaw of using engine fuel as the torque-converter medium, but otherwise all three types worked well enough within the typical British Railways operating regime.

The 'Blue Pullmans'

One further trainset must be dealt with at this stage, primarily because of the choice of engine but also because of the sets' historical significance.

The BTC Chairman's conference on modernisation during September 1956 referred to the concept of a self-powered Pullman train. Where did the idea originate? The minutes of the BTC Technical Committee in January 1955 reveal that den Hollander was invited to comment on the use of multiple-units in substitution for locomotive-hauled trains. He had been a leading figure in the introduction of such trains on the Continent, in the form of the 'Trans-Europe Express' sets. These were First-class only, aimed at the business market as a competitor to cross-border air travel between key cities, and they had a power car at each end.

A meeting on 10 March was supportive of the use of 'multi-unit diesel or diesel-electric express trains, an elaboration of the proposed inter-city trains for important runs from London to the North'. The 11 diesel-hydraulic locomotives from NBL could be used on sleeping-car services. The issue of terminology for publicity purposes brought a decision at the Committee meeting on 9 February 1956 to drop the term 'diesel multiple-unit' in favour of 'diesel trains', 'diesel express trains' and 'diesel-electric express trains'.

A committee under the chairmanship of H. H. Phillips, Assistant General Manager on the Western Region, and including among others R. C. Bond, as British Railways CME, submitted a report dated July 1956. Having considered the use of underfloor and bogie-mounted engines, the committee came down in favour of an arrangement similar to that of the Hastings sets, with engines above the floor. Two options were put forward, both using the 1,000hp MAN engine ordered from NBL as part of the contract for the first 11 diesel-hydraulic locomotives. Concerning the transmission, one option was for GEC electrical machines, while the other was for a

Voith hydraulic arrangement; the diesel-electric powertrain would weigh 49 tons and the diesel-hydraulic version 28½ tons. Although the Pullman Car Co general manager had affirmed the suitability of the concept for Pullman designation, there was as yet no plan for the trains to be so branded.

The LMR wanted two six-car sets for a First-class-only St Pancras–Manchester Central service, while the Western Region wanted three eight-car sets with first- and third-class seating to operate between Paddington, Bristol and Wolverhampton. At the 1956 Chairman's conference, the Eastern Region was invited to consider putting up a submission for a Marylebone–Sheffield train. By that date design considerations had come down in favour of diesel-electric drive, though it was noted that the consequent extra weight over hydraulic drive might make the planned Western Region schedules impracticable for an eight-car consist.

Approval for the sets came on 21 November 1956, the Metropolitan-Cammell Carriage & Wagon Co Ltd being contracted to build the mechanical parts.

There followed a lengthy gestation period before the first set emerged during early 1960. An editorial in *Diesel Railway Traction* for July 1960 was critical of the concept, citing the gross train weight of 299 tons for 132 passengers in the LMR sets as uneconomic. Interestingly, the editorial gives the total power as 2,380hp. Comparison was made to the heaviest German TEE seven-car sets of 1957 construction, which conveyed 105 First-class passengers and grossed 210 tons, with 2,670hp of engine power provided.

The editorial brought a swift riposte from Metropolitan-Cammell, which explained that the 'Midland Pullman' sets had two kitchen cars to provide a full at-seat meal service, whereas the TEE sets had only limited catering facilities, served from a single kitchen.

The German TEE sets were seven seven-car units, which were already under construction in September 1956 when the British Pullman sets were being schemed out. Their power equipment was the same as in the 'V200' locomotives, with either a Maybach MD650 or a Daimler-Benz MB820Bb 1,100hp engine in a power car at

The most prestigious DMUs were the five 'Blue Pullman' sets. This the leading power car of one of the two six-car sets used initially on the 'Midland Pullman'. *Sam Lambert*

The Western Region's duties for its new Pullman sets included services between Paddington and the West Midlands. This 1963 view features an eight-car set on arrival at Birmingham Snow Hill. *Rail Photoprints*

each end of the consist, coupled to either a Voith LT306r or a Mekydro hydraulic transmission. Top speed was 87mph.

The choice of power equipment for the British diesel Pullmans was interesting in itself. Each power car (two per set) had a MAN L12V18/21S engine, rated at 1,000hp at 1,445rpm. These engines are said to have been built in Germany rather than by NBL, which seems most curious in view of the BTC's aversion to importing power equipment from Germany for the Western Region diesel-hydraulics. The engine drove a GEC main generator, which powered four GEC traction motors. Top speed was 90mph.

Being required for high-value, prestige services, the 'Blue Pullmans' were accorded priority in maintenance and were provided with a riding technician, whose presence undoubtedly contributed to reliability by his being able to identify incipient problems before these became serious. Nevertheless, the MAN engines did give trouble, though less than was being experienced with the equivalents installed in the Western Region's locomotive fleet. A further factor in the improved engine performance is likely to have been the slightly lower rating than the 1,100hp of the locomotives, because peak cylinder pressures and temperatures would have been lower and hence less critical.

The service between Manchester and London was inaugurated on 4 July 1960, but the Western Region did not begin its service until 12 September. Once West Coast electrification was completed as far as Manchester in 1967 the two LMR sets joined the other three on the Western Region.

10

SEE HOW THEY RUN

As we head into the 1960s it is worth updating the world situation concerning locomotive power. In 1960 the world's most powerful locomotive, at 3,300hp, was *Deltic*, which employed two 1,650hp engines. The most powerful diesel-hydraulic locomotive was the 'ML3000' of 3,000hp, which had two Maybach MD655 engines of 1,500hp each. Both locomotives had engines running at a maximum of 1,500rpm. By contrast, the most powerful American-built locomotive was the General Motors SD24, which drew 2,400hp from one medium-speed diesel engine. This state of affairs prompted the Southern Pacific Railroad to take delivery in 1961 of six 4,000hp locomotives from Krauss-Maffei, which included twin Maybach MD870 diesels and the Voith L830rU torque-converter in the powertrain. With 29- or 30-ton maximum axle loads on the principal routes, and a very generous loading-gauge, the railways in North America faced fewer of the issues confronting their Western European counterparts, especially those in Britain.

Performance in service

Consideration must now be given to BR's experience with the diesel locomotives described in Chapter 8.

The 'D200s' were delivered between March 1958 and September 1962. While the first few worked primarily in East Anglia out of Liverpool Street, they were not popular with the Eastern Region for duties on the East Coast main line, because of the installed power of only 2,000hp. The next batch went to the LMR for West Coast work, and later builds were shared with the North Eastern and Scottish Regions. All four regions used the type to a greater or lesser degree for mixed-traffic duties, though even by 1959 the limited power available was seen as a handicap for top-link passenger activity. With the advent of the 'D1500s' the class was cascaded to lesser passenger turns, such as along the North Wales coast, and put in an increasing mileage on a wide variety of freights and the extensive parcels traffic. The majority of the class survived into the 1980s, concentrated increasingly on the LMR.

Strictly speaking, the BR/Sulzer Type 4 comprises three classes — the 'D1s' of 2,300hp and the 'D11s' of 2,500hp (both with Crompton Parkinson electrical equipment) and the 'D138s' of 2,500hp (with Brush electrical equipment). Construction began early in 1959 and was completed in January 1963. They were primarily the workhorses of the former Midland lines, which radiated from Derby to Bristol, London St Pancras, Manchester Central, Leeds, Glasgow St Enoch and York. The first series were quickly deemed non-standard and allocated to Toton (Nottingham) for freight-only operation, but the remainder were very much mixed-traffic. As the 1960s progressed, the 'D138' series migrated to North Eastern and Western Region depots, eventually finding regular employment as far afield as on Cornish clay branches and freights in the Home Counties, as well as along the East Coast to Edinburgh. Although, as with the 'D200s', the Eastern Region did not want the type for the East Coast, the installed 2,500hp made the fleet suitable for general express and a range of freight work, possibly the only handicap being the 90mph speed ceiling, ruling them out of the very top tier of services. Although the 'D1s' succumbed by about 1980, the others survived until the mid-1980s, when new freight traction and 'Sprinter' DMUs squeezed them out.

Of the diesel-hydraulics, No D600 underwent trials during late 1957 but was not accepted into stock until January 1958, the last of the NBL order for five locomotives being completed a year later. Most of the miles run were between Paddington, Plymouth and Penzance, and to a limited extent also Bristol. Well-known railway engineer and commentator O. S. Nock rated the class superior to the 'D800s', not least because of the ride quality. Nevertheless, judged non-standard by the Western Region, all five were withdrawn in December 1967.

The three original 'D800s', which had been ordered under the Pilot Scheme, were also judged to be non-standard with their sisters. No D800 *Sir Brian Robertson* was in traffic by

August 1958, and No D870 *Zulu*, the last of the Swindon build, emerged in October 1961. The NBL locomotives (Nos D833-65), with MAN/Voith powertrain in place of Swindon's Maybach/Mekydro, were delivered between July 1960 and June 1962, the last two after the company's liquidation. The locomotives' small wheels and light weight, which imposed a limit on locomotive brake force, ruled out their use on unfitted freights, and this brought deployment largely on passenger turns. These were not only on routes out of London but also on the Plymouth–Shrewsbury corridor. Regional boundary changes in 1962 saw more than half the Waterloo–Exeter route transferred to Western Region control, while in 1964 came a change of train haulage from Southern Region steam to the 'D800s'. By now it had become evident that the MAN engines were less reliable, especially when worked at full power. When the Western Region declared a surplus of 20 Type 4s in 1967 it was the NBL examples that were put up for offer, but without any takers, and after a short period on mixed-traffic work between London and Birmingham withdrawals commenced in 1969. The previous year had seen the demise of Nos D800-2, but the production series of Swindon-built locomotives now enjoyed something of a renaissance, as a result of the double-heading of the principal West of England services. Although this enabled schedules to be cut, it was expensive and did not last long. The run-down began in earnest during 1970 and was complete by the end of 1972.

Construction of the 'D1000' class began in the autumn of 1961 and continued until April 1964, Swindon's No D1029 *Western Legionnaire* completing the build. Initial duties were between Paddington and Wolverhampton Low Level (later extended to Chester) while the West Coast main line was undergoing electrification. Next came a takeover of South Wales services, and the class gradually spread across the whole region, though boundary changes brought an insistence by the LMR on the substitution of the 'D1500' class on the Birmingham route from January 1964. The class was the mainstay of the Western Region's internal Class 1 work for many years, as was reflected in average

annual mileages of 100,000 and more. The widespread introduction of electrically heated coaching stock during the 1970s began to narrow the services that could be covered, and this saw a switch to more freight utilisation, especially on Westbury stone traffic. British Railways' desire to close Swindon Works and the availability of alternative diesel-electric Type 4s sealed the fate of this last-surviving diesel-hydraulic class by February 1977.

The 'D1500' class was introduced in November 1962, all early examples being allocated to the Eastern Region for East Coast work alongside the 'Deltics'. The 512th example was completed during February 1967, by which date even the Southern Region had a few on its books. Over time the class came to be used almost anywhere from Inverness to Penzance. It is perhaps not widely understood that, until the advent of Type 5 freight traction in the second half of the 1970s, typically 70% of the utilisation was on freight, and the wide sphere of depot allocation and crew familiarity made the standard Type 4 truly a locomotive without frontiers. The run-down started in the 1990s, brought on by East Coast electrification, the spread of new multiple-units and the arrival of new freight power. Nevertheless, even at the time of writing, a few examples continue to find a role on passenger charters and selected freight work.

English Electric's 'D6700' class was built between December 1960 and November 1965. Initial deliveries were to East Anglia and the North East, but the Western Region took more than half the final total for South Wales, where the 'D6700s' worked almost exclusively on freight, either singly or in multiple, this dispensing with the WR's requirement for a heavy-freight locomotive. The North Eastern Region too generally confined its stud to freight work, while the arrival of the 'D1500s' in East Anglia meant that virtually no passenger work was covered. The Scottish Region received a small allocation in the 1960s for freight in the Central Lowlands, but motive-power rationalisation during the 1970s and 1980s brought increasing numbers north of the border, with passenger services diagrammed as far north as Wick and Thurso. Although a gradual run-down of the class began in the 1990s, around 30 were still in traffic in 2010.

The Hymek consortium had received an intimation that several hundred of its Type 3 design would be ordered in due course, but the final total was only 101. No D7000 entered traffic in May 1961, and No D7100 in February 1964. Intended for secondary mixed-traffic duties, the class quickly found itself on Class 1 diagrams between Paddington and South Wales, where they could keep timings based on even the largest steam engines. When problems with Type 4 diesel-hydraulics caused large-scale temporary withdrawals the 'Hymeks' stood in again on the South Wales and Bristol routes. By the start of the 1970s the only regular Class 1 diagrams were between Paddington, Worcester and Hereford. Run-down began around this time, partly because of loss of traffic, partly because Type 4 diesel-electrics had become available, and partly because of the desire to close Swindon Works. The last 'Hymeks' were retired in March 1975.

NBL outshopped No D6100 in December 1958, No D6157 completing the order in December 1960. Although the first 38 went new to Eastern Region depots in the London area their performance was so bad that all were packed off back to Scotland so that NBL could carry out modifications and rectification. The entire class was then allocated to depots in Glasgow or Aberdeen for mixed-traffic duties, though continuing poor reliability saw them displaced from passenger duties. By the mid-1960s roughly half the class was laid up out of use. Meanwhile, during 1963, No D6123 had a Paxman Ventura 12-cylinder engine, rated 1,350hp at 1,500rpm, substituted for the MAN diesel, and between 1965 and 1967 a further 19 of the class were similarly converted. A declining requirement for Type 2 power in the late 1960s saw all the class phased out by the end of 1971.

The 'D6300s' were built concurrently with their diesel-electric counterparts, delivery commencing in January 1959 but not being completed until November 1962, after NBL's liquidation. The six ordered under the Pilot Scheme had different locomotive-control arrangements, which meant that they could not work in multiple with their sisters and caused them to be confined to Devon and Cornwall. The class was popular on freights in Cornwall, where drivers appreciated the strong pulling ability. Although primarily a West Country machine, by virtue of its being the WR's standard Type 2, the class was also allocated to the Bristol and London areas for a range of work but excluding passenger trains. Rationalisation of BR's Type 2 fleet also saw the 'D6300s' succumb from the late 1960s, the final withdrawals being in 1971.

No more diesel-hydraulics?

In the minds of enthusiasts the Western Region's desire to opt for diesel-hydraulic traction arose for two reasons. First, it enabled the Western Region to continue to be different from other regions and so maintain the old Great Western Railway tradition. Even in the post-nationalisation golden era of Area Board independence (from 1953 to about the end of the decade) a region still had to obtain BTC approval for any scheme. This involved scrutiny by the BTC Central Staff, and the figures had to stack up; even repainting Western Region coaches in GWR chocolate-and-cream livery had to be sanctioned by the BTC. While there might have been a glint in the eye of some former GWR staff at the notion of daring to be different, in truth this was more dream than reality where serious money was involved.

The other reason put forward by enthusiasts for the choice of diesel-hydraulic was its superiority in tackling the heavily graded section of line between Newton Abbot and Plymouth, which was without parallel on any other major route. The lower continuous-rating speed of the hydraulic transmission was said to be the key. But no mention of this as a factor has been found in any official document or technical paper discussing the topic. What *has* emerged from technical papers has been the importance of adhesion — the ability of a locomotive to avoid slipping to a stand. Granted, the Western Region wished to remove the need for double-heading over the South Devon banks, but did the prevailing designs favour the diesel-hydraulic classes? Some figures from the Western Region's train-load-limit book for 1966 make interesting reading (see table).

Class loadings between Newton Abbot and Plymouth

Diesel type	Unassisted load (tons)
D10xx	550
D15xx	550
D11-193	490
D8xx	420
D70xx	365
D67xx	305
D6306-57	225

If the lower continuous rating of hydraulic traction was the alleged key determinant for the Western Region, there should have been a clear advantage in the maximum unassisted loads that these diesel types were permitted over this taxing route. These figures give the lie to this idea.

Having addressed the myths of why the Western Region wanted diesel-hydraulic motive power, we can now usefully repeat the comments of E. S. Cox, who ended his career as the British Railways Deputy CME under J. F. Harrison, already referred to in Chapter 7. The Western Region had no experience of electric transmission, and the use of hydraulic drive would avoid the need to enlarge its electrical side, which 'led them to welcome the suggestion that they should have the proposed diesel-hydraulic locomotives'. The BTC wished to try hydraulic drive, so confining the trial to one region was sensible, and the Western Region was the best choice.

Why did main-line diesel-hydraulics cease to be ordered? A clue can be found in a submission by Roy Hammond, the Western Region's General Manager in 1959, concerning the ordering of the 'D1000' class. He accepted that future orders for traction crossing regional boundaries would need to be diesel-electrics, because of the cost of training other regions in the operation and

The 'D6300' was the Western Region's standard Type 2 throughout the 1960s and saw service in the London, Bristol and Plymouth divisions. Piloting trains beyond the capacity of a 2,200hp Type 4 over the South Devon banks was a regular turn, and here No D6331 assists 'Warship' No D868 *Zephyr* with the up 'Cornish Riviera Express', photographed passing Laira Junction on 30 August 1961. *R. C. Riley*

maintenance of hydraulic drive. Nevertheless, the Western Region would have required additional Type 4 power for its yet-to-be determined Area 3 (Wales) scheme.

At a conference on railway modernisation in May 1962, J. F. Harrison read a paper in which he explained the decision to order no more main-line diesel-hydraulics, which was soon to be announced. He makes it clear that the urgent need for rapid dieselisation meant ordering a multiplicity of designs, and that by 1962 it had become necessary to standardise on as few designs as possible. Harrison stated that neither form of traction had demonstrated an advantage over the other and that both had proved perfectly capable of providing good performance and service, while there was no significant difference in the average transmission efficiency. There had been teething troubles with individual makes, but these did not represent fundamental drawbacks of either system. Although the diesel-hydraulics had a slight advantage in weight, the trend on cost appeared to have gone the other way. Apart from the Western, other regions were geared up for the maintenance of electrical machines, and it seemed likely that, on the world stage, this form of propulsion offered greater potential for future development.

Outlining issues affected both types of transmission, Harrison explained that close supervision during manufacture, particularly where this was undertaken under licence, was a key determinant in component reliability of both electrical machines and torque-converters. Provided this was proposed, the equipment had proved to be relatively trouble-free. Problems with control equipment had been the cause of 23% of diesel-electric locomotive failures and 40% for diesel-hydraulics. Reliability varied across the regions but averaged between 17,000 and 22,000 miles per casualty (mpc), comparable to steam's 17,000mpc.

Of relevance in relation to the relative economics of steam versus diesel are some comparisons by Harrison. He provided all-up costs for a Class 7MT 'Britannia' steam locomotive of Riddles design (the most modern in this power range) and a British Railways Type 4 2,300hp diesel-electric. Surprisingly, the break-even mileage was 40,000, while at 62,000 miles the diesel offered an economy over steam of 20%. These figures are interesting in the light of the Railway Executive's decision in 1952 that no advantage was to be gained by opting for main-line diesel traction instead of the modern steam locomotives being built at the time in British

Having gained Rail-blue livery and full yellow ends (and lost its 'D' prefix following the cessation of main-line steam working), No 6338 stands at Liskeard with an up van train on 13 July 1971. *G. F. Gillham*

Old Oak Common's allocation NBL Type 2s found employment on empty-stock moves at Paddington. No D6340 is seen arriving at the terminus on 25 April 1969. *Ian Allan Library*

Railways' workshops. According to Harrison, part of the shift in the cost balance of advantage lay in the rising cost of coal and the falling cost of oil during the decade to 1961.

Shortly after this paper was read British Railways announced that all future main-line diesels would have electric transmission. Summarising, in September 1954, R. C. Bond, the then British Railways CME, had put forward a case for trying diesel-hydraulic traction. This had come about, and it had worked as well as diesel-electric power, but, eight years on, it offered no advantage that would justify continued orders at a time when British Railways wished to develop as small a range of standard types as possible, on the grounds of economy of operation and maintenance.

Testing times

During October 1958 the Swindon Outdoor Testing Section conducted controlled road trials with No D801, which, as one of the three prototypes, was of nominal 2,000hp. A top speed of 103mph was achieved. The total engine output was assessed as 1,980hp at 1,400rpm, with 1,909hp input to the transmission. Peak transmission efficiency was 82½% between each gear change, slightly below that measured with No 10203. High transmission efficiency was obtained at the upper end of the speed range, making the design very suitable for express passenger work.

Separate trials on the South Devon banks demonstrated that restarts from rest, which demanded a factor of adhesion greater than 27.6% (48,000lb tractive effort), were difficult. As a result a 24% adhesion factor was judged to be the practical limit, with 42,000lb tractive effort for a 'D800' with full fuel and water tanks. The continuous rating was assessed as 12mph.

During 1961 trials with a 'D11'-class locomotive, to determine its haulage capacity on freight, established a maximum tractive effort of 65,000lb, roughly equal to 27.6% adhesion for a 140-ton locomotive with six of the eight axles driven. Prototype No D0280 *Falcon* was tested during 1962, when it achieved a maximum tractive effort of 70,300lb — 27.5% adhesion factor for a six-axle locomotive of 114 tons.

In 1965 the department of the BR Chief Officer (Traction & Rolling Stock) produced a report dealing comprehensively with its experience with the two types of transmission. The conclusion reached was that the balance of advantage was in favour of electric for British Railways' particular operating conditions. Of interest is the explanation as to why the Western Region favoured hydraulic drive — essentially this was because of observation of its operation in Germany, the high power-to-weight ratio and the fact that there would be no need to set up an electrical-maintenance department; there was no mention of the South Devon banks or low continuous-rating speed.

The following table summarises the results (set out more fully in the report) of comparative trials with a 'D1000' diesel-hydraulic and a 'D1500' diesel-electric.

	'D1000'	'D1500'
Maximum tractive effort	65,900lb at 4mph	71,700lb at 6.5mph
Adhesion factor	28% for 108 tons locomotive weight	27.4% for 117 tons locomotive weight[a]
Continuous rating	45,800lb at 13mph	30,000lb at 27mph
Transmission efficiency	59%	79%

[a] *Based on a locomotive weight of 117 tons, which is the weight usually quoted, though the report quotes 114 tons.*

Although the 'D1500' was able to sustain a steady 2,250rhp between 30 and 80mph (the generator unloading point) the peak rail horsepower of the 'D1000' – 2,170rhp – was produced at 55mph, this being the lowest speed at which the maximum engine speed of 1,500rpm was achieved.

The middle-range torque-converter was clearly better matched to the engine than the converters covering the low and high train-speed ranges, in which the capacity of the transmission exceeded that permitted from the engine and was limited by the actual supply to the traction rating of the engine. In the low- and high-speed ranges, nominal full power engine speeds balanced at slightly below 1,500rpm, with the fuel rack fully open, resulting in around 2,000rhp across most of the speed range. This issue will be discussed more fully later.

According to the report the 'D1500' transmission was specified by British Railways to optimise power at high speed, which resulted in a high continuous rating. Although the report claimed that this was not a problem for BR operations, it proved to be so within a few months of the report. The report goes on to say that such tuning of the transmission for a low continuous-rating speed with the 'D6700s' enabled them to match that of the 'D7000' diesel-hydraulic at around 12mph.

The 'D6700s' had identical traction motors and motor gear ratio to the 100mph 'Deltics', which had a continuous rating of 32½mph.

Although the main generator can be tuned to a particular characteristic, part of the reason for the low continuous rating with the 'D6700s' was that the engine output was low, relative to the capacity of the main generator. After all, the continuous rating is the speed at which full engine output can be absorbed continuously, so the higher the engine output for a given main generator, the higher must be the speed at which the continuous rating point is reached. The usual way in which designers of diesel-electric transmissions obtain a low continuous speed is by adjusting the traction-motor gear ratio, as was done in the late 1980s with the Railfreight Class 50, No 50 149.

Reverting to the report's findings, the transmission efficiency between engine and rail at speeds above 30mph was 81-82% for the diesel-electric and 74-77% for the diesel-hydraulic. As predicted in Chapter 5, the diesel-hydraulic had a higher locomotive specific resistance, owing to the transmission connection from engine to wheels, though the interconnection of axles on a bogie was found to offer better adhesion during poor rail conditions.

In correspondence on the issue of 'D1000' transmission efficiency, Voith's Wolfgang Paetzold has kindly provided a copy of the original hand-written acceptance test result for L630rV No 11523, which was supplied by Heidenheim as part of the order on Voith from NBL for 60 transmissions. Unfortunately the quality of the copy does not permit its reproduction here. Herr Paetzold has, however, deduced the following maximum efficiencies from the graph:

Starting torque-converter — 81%
Centre torque-converter — 86%
Third torque-converter — 82%

Paetzold states that Voith usually deducted another 3% for losses in axle drives and cardan shafts. For the 'D1000s', with their additional distributor gearbox, he would have deducted 5% altogether, and that would result in overall transmission efficiencies (from engine to driving wheels) of 76%, 81% and 77% respectively for the three torque-converters. Clearly the test results obtained

Pictured c1967, an unidentified 'D6300' heads up the former down line between Salisbury and Exeter, this section of the erstwhile SR main line to the West having been singled following its transfer to WR control.
Ian Allan Library

by British Railways were not dissimilar from what Voith would have expected.

A paper read by Rolf Keller, head of Voith Turbo's traction department, to the Institution of Locomotive Engineers, together with the subsequent discussion, provides further insight to this issue. Over the complete locomotive speed range there was a considerable variation in the input power demand of the transmission. It could vary from –10% at stall to +6% at maximum speed, corresponding to –127hp and +76hp for each transmission. In consequence, at some speeds the diesel was offloaded, while at others it was overloaded, with engine speed reduce to below 1,500rpm. This had the effect of reducing power input to the transmission by at least 3% below the nominal. Again, this confirms British Railways' test results with a 'D1000'. Keller acknowledged that the wide variation in the power consumption of the L630r was connected with the design of the converter rotor and some assembly factors.

The discussion also considered the characteristics of the governor of the Maybach MD655 engine and matching these to the transmission. Diesel engines driving electrical machines had more sophisticated governors than those used to power hydraulic transmission, in order to deal with the fluctuating load imposed on the engine by the generator. With a view to addressing these fluctuations, the governor design for such engines included 'governor droop', which was the change in engine speed from full load to no load, with the engine speed setting remaining at maximum. Of the engines used in Britain in conjunction with hydraulic drives, the MD655's governor had a droop of at least 150rpm, whereas the MAN L12V18/21 engine governor was isochronous (no droop). Keller agreed that the maximum torque conversion demanded during 'D1000' operation was higher than on other locomotives, because it had a small engine output relative to its total weight. This proved that the task of the transmission would have been easier with a more powerful locomotive, not a larger size of transmission. Keller's remarks are surprising, because the MD655 rating of 1,350hp matched the maximum input value of 1,300hp set by Voith for the L630.

How significant was the inferiority of the 'D1000s' on the road, when compared with

There is no doubt that the diesel-electric 'D6100s' were far less successful than their diesel-hydraulic counterparts, but the risk of a failure was not why, for a short time, the Scottish Region opted to pair up the class on the three-hour Glasgow Buchanan Street–Aberdeen expresses and also some Dundee services. On 23 February 1961 the 1.15pm to Dundee passes Robroyston West Junction, with No D6116 leading. *S. Rickard*

the 'D1500s'? Data collected during the 1960s on journeys between Paddington and Birmingham revealed that a 'D1500' was 5mph better climbing Hatton Bank than a similarly loaded 'D1000'.

A table of build costs in the 1965 report quotes £125,000 for a 'D1500' and £136,000 for a 'D1000' class. Curiously, the cost of a 'D6700' is given as £83,250, while a 'D7000' cost £87,950, a balance of advantage in no way corroborated by the tenders accepted in the years 1959-62 (and reported in Chapter 8). The latter, acquired in three batches, were never tendered above £80,000; and, accepting the first tender, reference was made specifically that it was lower than for English Electric's 'D6700s'. Was there some massaging of figures in the report?

The report includes availability figures up to October 1964. They cover a rather black period for the 'D1000s', while the great fall from grace of the 'D1500s' was yet to begin. For the Type 3s, the 'D6700s' attained an excellent 90½%, as against 83% for the 'D7000s'. Reliability in miles per casualty from new was 8,500 for the 'D1000s', 11,000 for the 'D1500s', 31,000 for the 'D6700s' and 18,000 for the 'D7000s'. What needs to be remembered is that both the diesel-electric classes were still being built at this time. The following table (*below left*) summarises the casualties, by type, per locomotive in traffic for a 20-week period during 1964. It shows that although there were four times as many transmission failures by the hydraulics they accounted for only 12% of the total.

A significant statement in the report concerns the design of hydraulic transmission in Britain. Self-evidently, hydraulic transmission has more mechanical components than does electric transmission, and each component needs to be designed properly against actual cyclic conditions, but this was not done thoroughly for the British

	'D1000'	'D1500'	'D6700'	'D7000'
Number of locomotives	74	179	240	101
Engine	1.08	0.75	0.16	0.24
Transmission	0.26	0.09	0.01	0.22
Electrical equipment	0.41	0.50	0.15	0.11
Total	**1.75**	**1.34**	**0.32**	**0.57**

Left: As a result of various problems with the engine and generator set No D6123 was selected for a trial fitting with a Paxman Ventura engine and overhauled generator. The locomotive ran trials for two years from June 1963 before further locomotives were converted, its regular stamping-ground being the Aberdeen/Dundee route to Glasgow. It is seen here near Gleneagles on 29 February 1964, with the 10.00 from Dundee. *Norman Pollock*

Below: Later conversions received a modified livery and train-headcode boxes. By that time the class was judged reliable enough to take over some West Highland line turns. This official BR photograph, dating from 1968, depicts a Mallaig–Glasgow working at Loch Eilt. *BR*

Among the early duties assigned to the 'Hymeks' were passenger workings between Paddington and South Wales, on which they displaced steam. Here No D7010 approaches Reading with the up 'Red Dragon'. *Cecil J. Blay*

designs. The report admits to a lack of complete understanding at the time of the issue of torsional vibration in the powertrain, which caused excessive wear, and sometimes failure, of components such as cardan shafts. Additionally, careful measurement of torque variations on individual axles of the 'D1000s' found up to 70% fluctuation either side of the mean effort, even in good rail conditions without wheelslip or torque transfer. Variations between individual axles were never found to be in phase and, where the applied torque was low, the induced torques were found to contain the same, or even a greater, amount of variation.

According to the report, the prime cause of hydraulic transmission failure on British Railways was due to under-design. Despite the upgrading of components, long-term fatigue in parts subject to complex vibrational causes were not understood fully at the time. By contrast, this did not appear to be a significant issue in Germany, where the performance of the 'V200s' went from strength to strength

during the same period, as reported in Chapter 6. The electrical machines of the diesel-electrics attracted little specific comment because (in the two classes described in the report) they had given little trouble.

The report's conclusions raise several issues. To paraphrase these conclusions, diesel-electrics, as delivered to British Railways, were cheaper at first cost and more reliable than diesel-hydraulics. It was however admitted that, with the benefit of hindsight, lessons learned would mean that a new design of either type would probably show only a marginal balance of advantage between the two transmission types. In the final analysis, British Railways felt that the balance of advantage for its operating conditions lay with diesel-electric.

These conclusions appear very selective to prove a point. First, the decision at the time of the Pilot Scheme to order two identical locomotives, except for transmission, from NBL, was taken specifically to make it possible to compare electric and hydraulic drives; yet these Type 2 classes are glaringly omitted from the report. Whereas the Western Region had made a good fist of dealing with issues arising out of the 'D6300s', by the date of the report, half of the Scottish Region's 'D6100s' were in store, considered unserviceable, while a number of the remainder were being rebuilt with new engines *and* rehabilitated GEC electrical machines. That state of affairs would not have enabled the argument to come down in favour of diesel-electrics.

Then there is the cost of construction. NBL priced the Type 2 diesel-hydraulics lower than the diesel-electrics, and surely this must mean something. Then, just compare the cost of construction in railway shops with the prices charged by outside contractors until Crewe began building the 'D1500s'. There must also be a degree of scepticism about railway works' costings. Despite what the report says, the tenders to the Works Committee for the Type

3s of each type showed a distinct price advantage for diesel-hydraulic. So it should! There were no expensive main and auxiliary generators and traction motors, and the resultant smaller locomotive absorbed less metal in its mechanical parts.

While the report claimed to be objective, it was only as objective as its chosen parameters allowed it to be. Comments about engine problems (not reproduced above) came just before major stress fractures in the Sulzer LDA28C engines that led ultimately to a derating to 2,580hp. There was no mention either of the fact that during the first nine months of 1962 the Swindon-built Type 4s had averaged 73,400 miles (or 98,000 annual equivalent) and that No D830 had managed 80,130 miles. The contemporary 'D11s' and 'D138s' were far less active, and were heading for a refurbishment programme in the years 1965-7 to eradicate a number of design defects. If the report had been reprised two

By the autumn of 1962 the 'Hymeks' had taken over many goods workings. No D7008 was photographed near Cole on 15 September. *G. O. Richardson*

The 'Hymeks' found their way onto SR metals, initially from Bristol to Portsmouth and later from Reading to Redhill. Here, on 28 September 1963, No D7018 is seen leaving Dorking Town with the 10.45 ex Tonbridge, having taken over at Redhill. This locomotive has since been preserved by the Diesel & Electric Preservation Group on the West Somerset Railway. *A. G. Dixon*

years later, its findings would, of necessity, have been far less favourable to the Type 4 diesel-electric classes.

In December 1966 S. O. Ell read a paper to the Institution of Locomotive Engineers entitled 'Some Design Problems of Diesel Locomotives'. Ell had recently left the post of head of the Swindon Outdoor Testing Section and was thus well versed in issues relating to the Western Region's motive power. His unit had undertaken the road trials with the 'D1000s' and 'D1500s'. It is worth quoting from his introduction. In it he refers to the statement in the 1965 report, comparing the transmissions, that 'The prime cause of hydraulic transmission failure on BR has ... been under-design.' Ell clearly felt pretty upset by this, because he retorted: 'The object of this paper is to rescue some worthwhile diesel-hydraulic contributions from obscurity in the matter-of-fact findings of a widely distributed report that is unmarked by

inspired insight into the design problems of the present-day locomotive and foresight into the future.' These are strong words about a report produced by one's ultimate superior! Ell makes the point that developments in the primary vibration system — the rotating-mass system of engine and transmission up to the converter, or the engine/generator system — had probably already borne fruit in a current new diesel-electric design.

Transmission troubles

At a 1965 datum, what is it fair to say about the performance of transmission systems, which are the theme of this book? For the majority of the diesel-electric classes, notably those with Brush, English Electric and, in the main, Crompton Parkinson equipment, the electrical machines had been largely (but not entirely) reliable.

The performance of the six-pole EE526 traction motor fitted in the 'D200s' proved prone to flashover on the LMR and, to a lesser degree, on the NER. These motors were exchanged for the four-pole EE551 motor, the cascaded machines being recycled into the last batch of 100 English Electric Type 1s. While the six-pole motors gave a superior torque curve, the use of six sets of brushes made them more prone to flashover on poor track than a four-pole motor of similar rating. By comparison, the 'D800', 'D1000' and 'D7000' classes all suffered some form or another of defect with the transmission, and these will be described in detail.

A further report produced by British Railways' CM&EE's Department in October 1965 catalogues 38 failures of electrical machines in the 'D1500s' during the previous three months, and two sets of traction motor modifications were carried out. A design change had already been introduced on the later-built locomotives, in which the traction motors were connected in an all-parallel arrangement, as compared with the series-parallel arrangement of the early batches. When withdrawals began after 1990, it was the series-parallel examples that went first, partly because they were the less reliable. No mention of these matters is made in the earlier report comparing the two forms of transmission, possibly because they were only emerging when it was written.

The condition of the track was an issue with the EE526 motors and the 'D1000' final drive. It is worth recalling the comments of the editor of *Trains Illustrated* during a visit to the Continent in 1959, in which he remarked specifically how much better the ride quality of the track was in the Netherlands and, especially, Germany. Whether track condition was a factor in traction-motor flashovers suffered by the 'D11s' is not known, though

'Hymeks' were never seen in large numbers west of Taunton and were very rare in Cornwall. By September 1970 line closures had brought track rationalisation at the former junction station of Norton Fitzwarren, where No 7002 was photographed at the head of a down train. *J. Reeves*

When regional
boundary changes put
the Lickey Incline within
its control the Western
Region wasted little
time in replacing steam
with diesel for banking
duties. English Electric
Type 3s were used
initially, before being
replaced by a pool of
four 'Hymeks', which
had the first
transmission range
locked out to prevent
any possibility of a gear
change during banking.
Nos D7023 and D7024
provide rear-end
assistance to freight on
17 October 1967.
A. A. Vickers

speeds above the permitted 90mph have usually been blamed.

The following more detailed remarks about specific locomotive classes are derived directly from papers presented to the Institution of Locomotive Engineers, from correspondence with Wolfgang Paetzold and from former Western Region engineers who had direct day-to-day experience of the WR diesel-hydraulics.

'D7000' class

The 'D7000s' suffered excessive wear on the splines of the main cardan shaft that linked the engine and transmission. Additionally, dynostarter auxiliary cardan shafts failed frequently, together with ruptures of the coupling in the pump branch. Investigation revealed unexpected severe vibration torques, and to suppress them the system was tuned, by reducing the engine/transmission torsional stiffness by a third and increasing by three the lumped inertia of the transmission. This was accomplished simply by inserting an additional coupling at the transmission end of the engine cardan shaft.

Defects in the K184 transmission control blocks led to malfunctioning of changes between the first and second transmission ratio (with consequential damage to the so-called cardan shaft No 5) and damage to gear teeth in the main gearbox. At first Maybach denied liability, but detailed study revealed that the designers had underestimated the high stresses caused by repeated shock loads. Research later carried out under Ell's supervision led to a redesign of both the shaft and the gear teeth at its extremity.

The transmission heat-exchangers became so hot that the solder that secured the oil tubes in position in the tube-plates escaped into the cooling-water system, from where it was difficult to remove. The solution was to substitute a solder with a higher melting-point.

'D1000' class

Looking at the 'D1000s' in his 1967 paper, Rolf Keller acknowledged that the design of hydraulic transmissions had evolved over the decade from 1952. Replying, T. Matthewson-Dick, Western Region CM&EE, commented that the modifications recommended to deal with primary and secondary vibrations came too late to save the 'D1000s' from real trouble in service, with considerable loss of reputation for the original designers; he added, however, that the control and electrical equipment had been at least as troublesome as the torque-converter and transmission generally.

Discussion on the paper continued on this theme, with a plea that transmission manufacturers should provide engine manufacturers with information about all the components in a transmission up to and including the driving element of the first converter, because the engine-maker was saddled with responsibility for completing a torsional study of the driving and driven machinery. It was speculated that no one was aware of the pitfalls when the earlier designs of transmission were in production. Replying from Voith's standpoint, Keller said that it was regarded as incomprehensible how Swindon overlooked the serious vibration conditions that arose in the Works' diesel-hydraulic designs.

In Ell's 1966 paper referred to above, Walter Jowett, a former English Electric engineer but by then with British Railways, commented that by then studies of torsional stress had been standard practice with diesel-electric designs for 20 years. Ell acknowledged that Swindon did not appreciate fully this issue. Manufacturers of both engines and transmissions were expected

In East Anglia the BR Standard Type 3s continued to operate passenger services on the King's Lynn route throughout the 1960s. Here one hurries the 15.25 to Liverpool Street through Audley End on 23 July 1969. *R. Elsdon*

Elsewhere the Type 3s were deployed almost exclusively on freight workings. On 13 December 1962 No D6730 comes off the Selby swing bridge with an up freight on the East Coast main line. *J. S. Whiteley*

to submit calculations to the sponsoring part of British Railways —in the case of the diesel-hydraulics Swindon Works. Systems based on such calculations needed to be checked at the prototype stage, to validate them in practice rather than in theory. Swindon recognised the importance of this process, but there was a rush to build the locomotives. Although Ell did not actually say so, it seems reasonable to infer, not least because of the various issues that arose in traffic, that the checking was in fact not done. No such issues arose with the Hymeks, which were built by Beyer Peacock.

Here one cannot help recalling the discussion back in 1959, when British Railways was ordering the 'D1000' powertrain. The Western Region opted to handle the design issues relating to marrying the components

itself rather than pay Bristol Siddeley, the engine manufacturer, to do so. One wonders whether the same issues would have occurred if Bristol Siddeley had co-ordinated the work.

Wolfgang Paetzold, in his history of Voith Turbo, summarises the 'D1000' transmission issues. Initially, the locomotives were plagued by many problems, notably in drive shafts and control systems, but over the years modifications improved matters. Whereas the German 'ML3000' C-C was designed to haul heavy freight at up to 100km/h (62mph), the 'D1000' class was designed to haul heavy passenger trains at high speed. Thus the 'D1000s' were extensively used at full load on poor, jointed track, and this caused problems, as did the redesign consequent on the need to relocate the powertrain in the middle of the

locomotive. These weaknesses were shown up particularly by the transmission linkage to the bogie, where vibration forces were also excessive. The rubber pads in the bogie assembly proved to be too small, and they wore away to leave metal rubbing on metal. Some bearings needed replacement after only 100,000 miles, bronze being substituted for brass. The ultimate solution would have been a redesign of the bogie.

Paetzold notes that, at mileages beyond 500,000, another failure occurred in the mechanical section. The hammering of the torque reaction rods with partly or totally destroyed rubber elements lead to wear and tear of the dog clutches of the reversing unit. The dogs (claws) on the inner and outer parts of each clutch had a 1.5° recess to keep the moving parts in position. This recess was subject to attrition whenever the locomotive was coasted at high speeds or run at part load, and eventually wore away. At these times the fluctuating torque in the secondary drive system was higher than the torque generated by the torque-converter turbine, causing the mating parts of the dog clutches to rattle. With the loss of the 1.5° recess, the selector ring of the dog clutch had to maintain the end position against axial forces. Heavy wear and tear on the selector rings was the result, and in several cases the transmissions had to be removed to fit new selector rings. As the cause of the inadmissible forces could not be eliminated — this would have necessitated a redesign of the bogie — the Western Region had to live with the wear and tear until the 'D1000s' were withdrawn.

EE Type 3 (Class 37) No D6857 skirts the south of Carlisle at Dentonholme North Junction with a Dalston–Tees Yard tank train on 2 April 1971. *Derek Cross*

The lack of locomotive brake force on the 'Hymeks' meant that the Western Region had to use diesel-electric English Electric Type 3s for South Wales freight traffic. Here No D6853 passes Briton Ferry with a short freight on 27 August 1963.
D. Wall

'D800' class

Although the equipment was a generation older in this design than in the 'D7000s', both of which had Maybach/Mekydro powertrains, it was the control gear that caused the greatest number of problems, whereas the Brush equipment in the 'Hymeks' was much more reliable.

'D833' class

Referring to the LT306r transmission used in the 'D800' and 'V200' classes, Rolf Keller explained that it had been designed for a specified partial load programme, and that problems developed only when the loading became higher or reached the peak; designs of the period of Keller's paper (1967) assumed peak loading. The MAN engine failures resulted in the 'D833' class's performing less reliably than the 'D800' class.

The Krauss-Maffei bogie

Krauss-Maffei wished to use the space normally occupied by the bogie centre pin to accommodate the drive system, and so designed a novel bogie arrangement. A virtual bogie centre was provided by a link and bell crank system, but there was no provision for lateral freedom, which, Ell commented, was provided traditionally and which in his view was dictated by first principles of bogie design.

Although the bogie rode well on the high-quality permanent way of DB, the irregularities of British Railways' track caused very rough riding with both the 'D800s' and the 'D1000s', which had the Krauss-Maffei design of bogie. Although the issue emerged before No D1000 itself took to the rails, it was too late to consider a new bogie design, and a solution had to be found for both types as quickly as possible. A number of modifications were carried out, including removal of the link and bell cranks. Instead, the body was suspended, with its lateral motion controlled by the secondary suspension links. Additionally, twin lateral hydraulic dampers were inserted in each bogie to absorb residual lateral oscillation. Tests of ride indices then shoed the 'D800s' and 'D1000s' to compare favourably with other BR diesel classes.

Cardan shafts

At the time, cardan shafts were used almost entirely in diesel-hydraulic designs, because in a diesel-electric locomotive the main generator was either coupled directly to the engine output shaft or connected via a gear drive, and power to the axle-hung traction motors was transmitted by cables. Particularly during the early days of hydraulic drive on British Railways, the importance of greasing the shafts, especially the universal joints, was not fully appreciated. When the splined sections were separated, it was essential that they were reassembled as before, with the same spines meshing, to retain the shaft balancing provided during manufacture; if the original matching was not preserved, vibration could damage the shafts and couplings.

Some performance figures

The presidential address given in 1967 by WR CM&EE J. Matthewson-Dick gave percentages of locomotives achieving at least 5,000 hours between overhauls at Swindon during 1966; these are shown in the following table.

Engine	Class	%
MD650	D800	65
MD870	D7000	60
MAN	D833	50
MD655	D1000	45

Regional policy was to change an engine, rather than work on it *in situ*, for anything

beyond minor work. Interestingly, it was not until 1967 that Swindon had a facility to test overhauled engines under load, and the lack of this was blamed for around 10% of engine failures that occurred in less than 1,000 hours. For a locomotive engaged primarily on passenger work this would be after about 25,000 miles, while the target of 6,000 hours was only 150,000 miles.

Transmission changes were planned at 12,000 hours — say 300,000 miles. Contrast this with the DB performance referred to in Chapter 6, which was significantly higher, annual mileages also being about 40% greater. Best performers were the L630 ('D1000') and K104 ('D800'), with about 40% running for the target interval, then came the K184 ('D7000') at 35%, and finally the LT306 ('D833') at 25%.

Causes of failure by percentage of defects, 1961

Cause of failure	Diesel-electric	Diesel-hydraulic
Bodies, underframes, bogies, wheels	0.8	–
Power unit and associated equipment	21.9	18.2
Pipework	14.8	9.1
Brakes	10.0	6.8
Other forms of braking	0.3	–
Train heating equipment	26.8	13.6
Hydraulic drive components	–	4.5
Generators and traction motors	2.6	–
Resistances, auxiliary machines, control and other equipment, including AWS and fire protection	22.8	47.8

Looking more generally at the causes of failure, the figures given in the table are illuminating. Although J. F. Harrison referred to them in his 1961 presidential address as 'teething troubles', Matthewson-Dick confirmed that the proportions remained roughly the same in 1967 and now had to be classed as 'deep-rooted'. In summary, roughly one third comprised control gear (often the protective devices), one third the engine (but only indirectly and mainly cooling systems), and most of the remaining third related to carriage-heating equipment.

Figures from the Spring 1967 timetable for target mileage per day per locomotive were 507.5 for the 'D1000s' and 307.9 for the

	'D6700'	*'D7000'*	*'D1500'*	*'D1000'*
Availability 1966	90%	80%	75%	65%
Actual mpc 1966	49,786	42,362	12,953	12,432
Forecast mpc 1970	64,000	67,000	23,000	42,000

The A1A-A1A 'Warships' soon came to be regarded as non-standard and were an early casualty of fleet rationalisation. Most of their short lives were spent plying between Paddington and the West Country. Here No D601 *Ark Royal* hauls at least 11 coaches on the up 'Royal Duchy', passing Langstone Cliff at Dawlish Warren on 29 July 1961.
G. H. S. Owen

'D1500s'; for the Type 3s it was 230.2 for the 'D7000s' and 144.2 for the 'D6700s', all reflecting differences in the types of train hauled.

During 1967 the British Railways CME produced two reports for the Board, one covering what were described as the major classes and the other the minor classes. These documents delineate the availability and reliability during 1966, technical issues confronting the engineers, and forecast performance by 1970. Reliability in miles per casualty for 1966 was as shown in the table above.

During 1966 the British Railways/Sulzer Type 4 variants averaged 10,029mpc, and the

English Electric 'D200s' 18,229mpc. The report summarises the position class by class. English Electric's Type 3 ('D6700' class) was one of the best performers, owing to a conservatively rated engine and the absence of steam generators in half the class. Problems with the 'D7000' transmission had been addressed by modifications carried out by the manufacturer, though there were still some minor engine problems.

Turning to the 'D1500s', apart from the serious engine issues that remained to be resolved at the time, the report acknowledges that 'many improvements found necessary' during six years of production had been incorporated, although much work remained to be done. The 'D1000s' were still suffering from engine and transmission issues, but modifications in hand were expected to resolve them.

The NBL Type 2s must not be overlooked, because they were intended to

Above: The English Electric Type 4 suffered from a low power-to-weight ratio. Despite this, it displaced the 2,300hp BR Type 4s on the more arduous West Coast main line, where the 10-mile assault of Beattock, with its 1 in 74 grades, was most taxing. On 9 June 1961 No D322 passes Quintinshill with an eclectic rake of at least 15 coaches forming the down 'Royal Scot', which will require assistance on the climb to Beattock Summit. *Derek Cross*

Below: The Stratford-based EE Type 4s had lighter loads on the London–Norwich expresses but were required to run regularly at speeds of up to 90mph, which at this time was uncommon on the West Coast main line, due to ongoing electrification work. Here No D202 leaves Norwich Thorpe for Liverpool Street on 12 September 1964. *J. S. Hancock*

provide a comparison between the two transmissions. Thirty of the 'D6100s' were in store, considered unserviceable, by March 1967, and those that were not earmarked for the refurbishment and re-engining programme were due for withdrawal. Even those that had been refurbished — the work including rewinding the main generator armature — were experiencing problems. By contrast, the diesel-hydraulic 'D6300s' had only minor problems with the transmission, and experiments under way with six of the 'D833s' were expected to improve engine performance.

In conclusion, locomotives with both types of transmission suffered problems, but they were more manufacturer-specific rather than generic. In theory a well-designed hydraulic drive should need minimal maintenance, consisting essentially in keeping it topped up with oil. The 'D7000s' worked as well as any comparable diesel-electric on

similar duties (which the 'D6700s' were not), so, clearly, locomotive design was a factor. NBL's locomotives were problem children, whatever their transmission. Sadly, so were Swindon's 'D1000s'; modifications over the years cured many defects in the design but could not eradicate them all. The 'D1500s', the so-called standard Type 4, hardly had 10 identical locomotives by the end of the 1960s, such was the range of modifications made.

Leaving politics aside, the demise of locomotives with hydraulic drive can, in the words of Western Region engineers, be put down to the cost of spares and overhauls carried out by Swindon, when compared with spares for other classes and work done in other British Railways shops. By the end of the 1960s British Railways appreciated that it would soon have sufficient diesel-electrics to allow the remaining diesel-hydraulics to be withdrawn and, in so doing, to end locomotive repairs at Swindon.

The EE Type 4s were useful freight locomotives, though not for the heaviest workings.
On 7 September 1964 No D308 sets off from Shap station on a Hardendale (Shap Quarry)–Motherwell working with limestone for steel manufacture in the Motherwell area. On the up line can be seen Ivatt '4MT' No 43029 on local shunting duties.
Derek Cross

Above: Even the 133-ton bulk of the English Electric Type 4 did not always provide sufficient practical brake force on some busy routes. To address this a brake tender acted as a fitted head, as on this unfitted coal train seen crossing Saddleworth Viaduct, on the Huddersfield–Stalybridge route, on 6 June 1967. *R. J. Farrell*

Left: This is an interesting view of Swindon that differs in so many ways from the present scene. The 'D800s' put in a lot of work on the Bristol road during their early years. On 20 May 1962 No D829 *Magpie* has the 12.30 Paddington–Weston-super-Mare in tow. *J. A. Fleming*

137

Above: During the latter half of the 1960s the Western Region tried several options for speeding up its train services beyond what a single Type 4 could achieve with prevailing loads. From 6 May 1968 eight West of England expresses were diagrammed for a pair of selected Swindon-built 'D800s'. A trial run was made with Nos D827 *Kelly* and D822 *Hercules* and featured in this official Western Region photograph. *BR*

Below: The small wheels on the first-generation Swindon Type 4s were recognised by early 1959 as a problem for braking unfitted trains, because the heat generated by the braking effort could not be dissipated quickly, and consequently the second-generation Type 4s, the 'Westerns', had larger wheels. Here 'Warship' D806 *Cambrian* rumbles westbound through Westerleigh, north of Bristol, with a parcels train. *G. F. Heiron / Transport Treasury*

Left: The low weight of the 'D800s' gave them an advantage in hauling passenger trains, especially over the South Devon banks. Here, in blue livery with full yellow ends, No D804 *Avenger* passes Aller Junction on an inter-regional working. *G. F. Gillham*

Below: Regional-boundary changes brought the SR line west of Wilton Junction, Salisbury, under Western Region control, and from September 1964 Swindon-built (but not NBL) 'D800s' displaced steam between Waterloo and Exeter. Here No D816 *Eclipse* is seen between Gillingham and Templecombe at the head of a westbound train comprising mainly SR stock. *Ivo Peters*

Right: As envisaged by J. F. Harrison, the LMR's CM&EE at the time of the Pilot Scheme order, the BR/Sulzer 'Peaks' were the principal Type 4s on the former Midland Railway routes that radiated from Derby, and as a result they penetrated as far north as Glasgow St Enoch via the GSWR line from Carlisle. On 1 June 1963 No D27 runs down to Dumfries at the head of a Glasgow–Leeds train, passing a Fairburn 2-6-4 tank at the junction with the 'Port Road' to Stranraer. *Derek Cross*

Right: As late as 1968 Bristol remained a point where inter-regional services either changed traction or terminated — a continuation of pre-nationalisation practice. On 9 March 'Peak' No D20 arrived in the city with the 08.15 from Newcastle and is pictured at Bedminster Park *en route* to Malago Vale carriage sidings with the empty stock. *David Wharton*

Left: The 'Peaks' also took quite a share in freight movements. Although the headcode suggests a train bound for the Liverpool Division the photographer identifies the working as heading south through Loughborough on 14 September 1965. *J. H. Cooper-Smith*

Below: Being BR's standard Type 4, the Brush 'D1500' class (better known by its TOPS designation, Class 47) was allocated to all the regions at some point. Early in 1967, prior to electrification to Bournemouth, even the SR had several on its books. Here No D1923 shares Bournemouth shed with a clutch of steam locomotives (including 'Merchant Navy' Pacific No 35013 *Blue Funnel*) on 26 March 1967. *Gavin Morrison*

Right: Even before the 1962 boundary changes the Western Region recognised (in 1959) that it would require a fleet of diesel-electric Type 4s for inter-regional services as part of the planned policy of through locomotive working. From January 1964 the LMR insisted that the BR/Brush Type 4 should replace the 'D1000s' on the Paddington–Wolverhampton route, and the Western Region received an allocation for this purpose. No D1711 leaves Knowle on Sunday 24 May 1964 with the 4.30pm ex Wolverhampton. *Michael Mensing*

Right: Although deployed initially on the Birmingham road, the Class 47s eventually came to dominate the diagrams from Paddington to South Wales, as well as appearing on Bristol and West Country services. No 1640's driver appears to have shut off for the Reading call on the 10.45 Paddington–Weston-super-Mare as it hurries through Sonning Cutting at around 90mph on 25 July 1970. *Author*

Above: It is not generally appreciated that roughly 70% of Brush Type 4 utilisation was on freight diagrams. No D1864, barely two months old, passes Ilkeston Junction station on 17 July 1965 with a rake of loaded coal wagons from its home Eastern Region, possibly bound for Toton, on the LMR.
J. S. Hancock

Left: It was on loaded merry-go-round workings between the Nottinghamshire collieries and West Burton power station that the high continuous-rating speed of the Class 47s proved critical, main generators burning out on the long, steady gradients because train speed was below what the generators could cope with for long periods. On 17 July 1974 Class 47/3 No 47 305 approaches Toton Yard with empties from Ratcliffe power station.
Philip D. Hawkins

Above: The 'Westerns' were the principal express-passenger locomotives on the Western Region until the mid-1970s. Here, on 17 April 1969, No D1007 *Western Talisman* approaches Twyford with the down 'Cornish Riviera Express' (10.30 ex Paddington). *G. P. Cooper*

Right: The driver and riding technician aboard No D1061 *Western Envoy* pose for the photographer as the locomotive at the head of a down express. *Cecil J. Blay*

Left: The 'Westerns' were never frequent visitors to the Cheltenham–Birmingham route, but on 10 June 1964 No D1017 *Western Warrior* found employment on an excursion from Bristol to Stratford-upon-Avon, being seen here at Honeybourne New Yard. *Derek Cross*

Below: The low continuous rating of the 'Westerns' made them ideal for the growing traffic from the Mendip quarries, and in their later years they were much employed in the Westbury area. On 1 April 1976 No 1033 *Western Trooper* waits for the road at Westbury with a Blue Circle cement train. *Philip D. Hawkins*

11

A DIVERGENCE THROUGH TRACTION APPLICATION

By the 1970s BR recognised that the mixed-traffic diesel was a dead concept and developed separate traction for high-speed passenger services and heavy freight, both with diesel-electric transmission. Here the two come side by side at Bristol Parkway on 2 November 1979, as an HST forming the 10.45 Swansea–Paddington passes Class 56 No 56 040 on a merry-go-round coal train for Didcot power station. *G. Scott-Lowe*

The end of the mixed-traffic locomotive

The decade from 1967 was to see further changes to the BR traction fleet. The omission of sanding gear from the 'D1500' class (henceforward known as Class 47) was found to have been a big mistake, causing operating problems in poor rail conditions where a 'D1000' (Class 52) or even a 'D11' (Class 45) with working sanding gear sailed along. Jeremy Clarke, a leading Western Region locomotive engineer, was in a position to assess the performance of the three types for the haulage of a train up Luxulyan Bank on the Newquay branch, ranking Class 52 first, Class 45 second and Class 47 third. Consequently the new Class 50 design had sanding gear on some of the driven axles, while later locomotive designs had full provision. Luxulyan Bank was the location of an incident worthy of mention. A Class 45 coping with a 14-coach train ascending the

bank towards Newquay burned out its main generator because the continuous rating was exceeded for too long a period. Consequently, trains of this size had a change to a Class 52 at Plymouth, because of the diesel-hydraulic's lower continuous speed.

Then there came the abandonment of the concept of the mixed-traffic locomotive, because it was recognised that the needs of the freight and passenger businesses had diverged to the point at which one diesel (but not electric) locomotive could fit the bill. Resulting from this was the evolution of what came to be the High Speed Train. The HSTs had a power car at each end, with a high-speed Paxman engine (the Valenta) that actually worked well! Brush had developed reliable AC power-generation equipment, and bogie-mounted DC traction motors. The maximum speed was 125mph, which contrasts with the 80mph limit of the Type 5 freight locomotives (Classes 56 and 58) that were produced in British Railways' workshops and elsewhere between 1976 and 1987. The freight locomotives also had Brush AC generators and DC traction motors, but their diesel engines used were developments of the English Electric CSVT range, which had evolved from Nos D10000 and D10001, through the 'D200s' and the 'D6700s'.

Hydraulic drive was, however, by no means a dead art in rail use, and some new designs did appear on the world stage, though expanding electrification was cutting back on the demand for diesel power. In the early 1970s, on the basis of experience with a pilot order, the People's Republic of China took delivery of thirty 5,400hp locomotives, built by Henschel and equipped with Voith transmission. 1968 was the peak year by value for Voith's rail division, 50% going for export. An order from SNCF (French National Railways) for transmissions for 300 shunting locomotives had to be turned down on capacity grounds, and it was in this sphere, along with railcars and small main-line locomotives, that hydraulic drive proved highly popular. Technical progress continued, with the production of more compact hydraulic drives. By contrast, the development of AC traction motors that could be used in squadron service to drive locomotives and railcars was some way off.

Chapter 10 referred to a paper read by Rolf Keller to the Institution of Locomotive Engineers in 1967. Although he did not elaborate on the solutions produced, Keller stated that between 1952 and 1962 the (hydraulic) transmission-design engineers addressed:

- Primary vibration between engine and transmission
- Axle-drive suspension and suitable torque arm links
- Cooling of transmission oil
- Secondary vibrations, including coupled bogies and gearwheels
- Roller bearings
- Overspeed and wheelslip problems

The foregoing invites the conclusion that, for locomotives rather than railcars, the effective inception of hydraulic drive in 1952 was only the start of a learning process that took a decade to complete. Prewar German experience had been confined to railcars — successfully so — but only a very few main-line diesel-hydraulic locomotives had been built.

Discussion of Keller's paper considered the suitability of diesel-hydraulic transmission for a mixed-traffic locomotive, with a speed range up to 100mph. The use of a coupling at the output side of the torque-converter was put forward, which would have made for a quasi-mechanical arrangement. The main issue with the approach was that engine manufacturers of the day (1967) severely restricted the operating speed range of the diesel engine at maximum torque. Matters had moved on by the 1980s, not least because mixed-traffic locomotives were a thing of the past, and also because of advances in engine design. This now moves the story to the second-generation DMUs that emerged in the 1980s, which eventually saw off virtually all timetabled diesel-locomotive-hauled passenger services.

Modern multiple-units

Technical improvements helped to ensure that diesel-hydraulic drives remained cheaper than diesel-electric. It was, however, a traditional DC traction-motor arrangement that British Railways chose in 1978 when planning the replacement of its fleet of first-generation suburban multiple-units. Having proved successful on the Southern Region, the model chosen was conceptually the same as the 'Hampshire' diesel-electric sets, using a body based on the new Class 317 EMUs. Two prototypes were produced, a four-car with an MTU diesel and Brush electrical equipment, and a three-car with a Paxman engine and GEC electrics. Delivered in 1982, these Class 210 sets of around 1,150hp were expensive — too expensive for the urban passenger transport executives that would be expected to contribute towards the cost of them. Equally, their high capital cost ruled them out of work on secondary routes such as the Cambrian and West Highland lines.

British Railways had to think again, and came up with a 'bus on wheels' — the Leyland National body and the Leyland/Self Changing Gears (SCG) diesel-mechanical powertrain. Built in several guises from 1983 as two-car sets, each with a single 200hp engine, and four-speed gearbox, these units were cheap to produce and were suitable for urban use outside London and on some secondary services. With only two axles, no

Right: The over-
specified (too expensive)
Class 210 diesel-electric
multiple-unit, which
was based on the
successful SR 'Hastings'
and 'Hampshire' sets.
BR

Right: The over-
specified (too expensive)
Class 210 diesel-electric
multiple-unit, which
was based on the
successful SR 'Hastings'
and 'Hampshire' sets.
BR

bogies, the ride quality on anything other than excellent track was poor. In time, the SCG gearbox proved not to be sufficiently resilient, and was replaced by a Voith hydraulic drive.

To meet the needs of other urban, inter-urban and cross-country services, British Railways contracted with its own workshops — by then British Rail Engineering Ltd (BREL) — and Metropolitan-Cammell for two prototype sets from each builder. These quickly formed the basis for Classes 150, 155, 156, 158 and 159, dubbed 'Sprinters', 'Super Sprinters' and 'Express Sprinters'. Built by several suppliers, they were fitted (in the main) with Cummins diesels of varying outputs, depending on the railcar type, and Voith T211 transmission, but with a direct drive from the

Right: Clearly
resembling the Leyland
National city bus from
which it was derived,
prototype railbus LEV1
is pictured at Derby on
30 May 1982.
P. H. Groom

Above: As a cheaper alternative to the Class 210 BR commissioned four prototype diesel-hydraulic units — two from Derby Works and two from Metropolitan-Cammell. The latter produced two Class 151s, of which No 151 002 is seen leaving Derby on 21 February 1987 as the 12.35 to Matlock. *W. A. Sharman*

Left: The Class 150 and 151 prototypes spawned the familiar 'Sprinter' series of diesel multiple-units, all with hydraulic transmission. Class 158 was geared for 90mph and dubbed the 'Express Sprinter'. On 11 October 1989 the first of the series, No 158 701, was undergoing trials between Derby and Leicester, being pictured here at Ratcliffe-on-Soar. *L. A. Nixon*

After privatisation there emerged several new designs of DMU, the majority continuing to employ hydraulic traction. One of the Class 175 'Coradia' units built by Alstom for First North Western, No 175 102 skirts the Carmarthen coast at St Ishmael while on a Milford Haven–Manchester Piccadilly service on 24 July 2006. *Author*

engine at speeds of more than about 45mph. Demonstrating the supremacy of Voith in this sector, Classes 141-144, 150, 155, 156, 158, 159, 165 and 166, most of Class 170 and Class 175 have a T211 transmission in several forms, while Classes 180 and 185 have the T312.

Class 172s have a ZF (Zahnradfabrik Friedrichshafen) hydromechanical transmissions. This incursion into what Voith seems to regard as hydrodynamic transmission territory prompted the company to put together a presentation setting out the advantages of its system over the perceived interloper and competitor. It has served to reignite the arguments of the 1950s, Voith and Mekydro both arguing the merits of their respective systems. While Voith acknowledges higher initial costs, it maintains that whole-life costs are lower for its transmission. Voith knows of no instance in which its transmissions have been replaced by a hydromechanical system, but quotes a number of instances where the reverse is the case.

Top speeds vary between 75 and 100mph, except for Class 180, which is permitted to run at 125mph. This proves that, finally, the

engine and transmission manufacturers had produced a powertrain, with a mechanical drive for the upper speed range, that gives the best mix of drive options for low and high speed. Recalling Herr Keller's paper, quoted above, this shows that, after 15 years' development, engine manufacturers were now able to offer high torque over a broad speed band. Looking at the tractive effort/speed and efficiency curves for the various 'Sprinter' units, in which direct drive is engaged around 45mph, it is evident that above this speed is where the highest efficiencies — more than 90% — are achieved. Additionally, the tractive effort/speed curve becomes much flatter as engine speed (and thus output) rises towards the maximum.

Of course, not all modern diesel units have hydraulic drive. The 'Voyager', 'Super Voyager' and 'Meridian' units of Classes 220, 221 and 222 are diesel-electrics. The same Cummins engine found in Class 180 was chosen, and this drives a generator that powers two body-mounted traction motors. The final drive to the axles is, ironically, of Voith manufacture!

Above: Forming the 11.56 Exeter–Paddington, No 180 110 heads east near Somerton on 9 February 2006. *Rail Photoprints*

Left: For its CrossCountry franchise operation Virgin Trains ordered two similar diesel-electric designs built at Derby — the Class 220 'Voyagers' and tilting Class 221 'Super Voyagers'.
A Birmingham–Glasgow Class 221 'Super Voyager' powers towards Winwick Junction on 11 December 2009. *Author*

In the present era of privatised railways in Britain there is much less disclosure of information than under British Railways. It does seem, however, that the Voith T211 system has proved to be generally trouble-free. An issue with the bearings on the transmission selector shaft has been resolved by a change of bearings.

A number of problems plagued the Class 180 'Adelante' sets built for Great Western Trains, mainly design-related. GWT took great care to impress upon the builders the need to avoid the reverse torques in the final drive that beset the 'D1000s', and this was achieved. With regard to the transmission, the solenoid switch, located inside the torque-converter, kept burning out, and this problem was addressed by changing the type of oil used, even though the original oil was on Voith's approved list. The oil pipe from the transmission alongside the engine to the heat-exchanger for oil cooling proved troublesome, being liable to rupture; this experience taught Voith a lesson to site the transmission-oil heat-exchanger next to the transmission in the subsequent Class 185 'Desiro' design. Finally, immediately after starting an engine, before the direction selection was completed, the transmission turbine was found to be 'windmilling' — spinning of its own accord — which prevented the selection of a direction

of travel to start the train. Again, this has been rectified.

On the road, however, Class 180 appears to have the edge over its diesel-electric counterparts. All these types employ the same model of diesel engine, but experience between Reading and Didcot, where Class 180 has performed alongside Class 220, shows superiority to the former. Moreover, Hull Trains has operated Classes 180 and 222, and that company's drivers consider Class 180 to be superior. It should, however, be recorded that, whilst Classes 220-222 have suffered some technical faults, the diesel-electric drive has not been reported as having any fundamental design flaws.

The drive for tractive effort

In the early 1960s J. F. Harrison, effectively the BR CM&EE (though this was not his official title), began work on a 4,000hp diesel. By 1965, with no possibility that British Railways would fund its construction, he was happy to hand over the project to Brush. Brush was developing AC power-generation equipment for rail application and in January 1968 completed construction of the 4,000hp prototype, HS4000 (named *Kestrel*). This used the Sulzer 16LVA24 engine, which monster helped push up the locomotive weight beyond the planned 126 tons to 133 tons on Co-Co

The most powerful diesel locomotive ever to run on British metals, Hawker Siddeley prototype HS4000 *Kestrel* is seen on shed at Cricklewood in July 1969. Its BR trials completed, it would be sold in 1971 for further use in the Soviet Union, where it was to survive until 1989. *D. A. Idle*

bogies, which was unacceptable for high-speed passenger service. Though referred to as a Brush project, there is evidence that Harrison continued to contribute to planning the design during the Brush phase.

What emerges from the *Kestrel débâcle* of a locomotive unwanted by the Operating Department? If Harrison had not set his face against quick-running engines and hydraulic drive, he could have had a 4,000hp locomotive as early as 1962, when Henschel produced the 'V320' for DB (see Chapter 6). In 1964 SNCF took delivery of a 4,800hp prototype with Voith transmission, which weighed just 82 tons and was mounted on two-axle bogies. In 1967 the People's Republic of China received four 4,000hp diesel-hydraulics, and RENFE (Spanish National Railways) was ordering prototypes of similar power. By the time HS4000 appeared there were a number of locomotives of similar or higher power in use worldwide, most of them with hydraulic drive.

Furthermore, Harrison's argument that, by 1962, the medium-speed diesel-electric could closely match the power-to-weight ratio of its hydraulic counterpart overlooked the simple fact that the latter had also progressed in design, ensuring that the gap was as wide as ever, as can be seen from events overseas. Where Harrison's report of 1965, comparing the two forms of transmission, did prove accurate was that diesel-electric drive offered greater potential for future development. British experience has shown that sheer horsepower was not the answer for freight haulage, and HS4000 remains the most powerful single-unit diesel ever to run on this country's metals.

Although hydraulic drive was cheaper to buy and maintain than electric, and so has proved popular for railcar use, the development of full AC electric drives finally became a possibility for locomotives. Alternating-current machines do not have the commutator and brush gear of DC equipment, and so eliminate a major source of maintenance and trouble. High voltages in DC motors at high road speed have often given rise to a high risk of flashover. This is not a problem with AC motors, which therefore have the advantage of a high-voltage, low-current traction supply, making it possible to use smaller conductors for the same power delivered.

The AC traction motor is a much simpler and consequently more robust item mechanically (and in some aspects electrically) than its DC equivalent, which is a big advantage, given the vibration and shock to which it is subjected in use. Theoretically the DC motor delivers maximum power at zero speed (in reality some issues get in the way of doing that), which is excellent for traction applications, giving maximum power just when it is necessary to accelerate a train from rest. Until recently AC motors gave maximum power at rated full speed, but at zero speed were very weak in comparison with DC motors. With the advent of highly controllable (and now reliable) power electrical components and advanced microprocessor control systems, coupled with sophisticated software models of the motor and the traction application, much of this shortcoming can be overcome.

In the freight sphere, high tractive effort means heavier trains and economy of operation. Traditionally, this came at the expense of high top speed, but during the 1980s locomotive manufacturers used advances in technology to improve the performance of the DC traction motor, using separately excited motors and wheel-creep systems, which offered both better wheelslip protection and tractive capability. These refinements, plus a further tuning of the electrical machines for the desired speed range, gave marked performance benefits. The following table offers a 50-year picture of evolution, right up to 2010. It helps to highlight the fact that Classes 56, 58 and 66/0-5 are intended for general freight utilisation. By contrast, Classes 59, 60 and 66/6 were designed for pulling the heaviest loads at moderate maximum speeds. Including Freightliner's General Electric Class 70 and Voith's first foray into locomotive design brings the story up to date. Class 70 sees the first application of an AC/AC transmission in a locomotive operating in Britain. Launched in 2007, the Voith Maxima would have been a contender for Freightliner's Class 70 project, if it had been further down the proving road and capable of being scaled down quickly for the British loading-gauge (*see table below*).

Looking at the continuous rating data and the motor gearing, it becomes clear how diesel-electric drive achieves the highest torque but at the expense of speed. Only in the three most modern types — Class 70 and the Maximas — has this become less of an issue, but only with the benefit of advancing technology.

Class	Introduced (in UK)	Engine output (bph)	Maximum speed (mhp)	Tractive effort (kN)		Speed (mph)	Gear ratio	Ratio to unity
				Maximum	Continuous			
47	1962	2,750	95	276	133	27	66:17	3.88
52	1961	2,700	90	297	201	14.5	*None*	*n/a*
56	1977	3,250	80	275	240	17	63:16	3.94
58	1983	3,300	80	275	240	17.4	63:16	3.94
59	1985	3,300	60	506	290	14	62:15	4.13
60	1989	3,100	60	502	336	11.7	97:19	5.11
66	1998	3,200	75	409	260	15.7	81:20	4.05
66/6	2000	3,200	65	467	296	13.7	83:18	4.61
70	2009	3,700	75	544	427	11.3	85:16	5.31
Maxima 40	-	4,850	75	519	460	9.5	*None*	*n/a*
Maxima 30	-	3,700	75	519	460	9.5	*None*	*n/a*

Note: The details in the table take no account of differences in wheel diameter.

Opposite page:
Class 56 No 56 013 accelerates its 36 loaded HAA coal hoppers through Worksop *en route* from Creswell Colliery to West Burton power station on 11 August 1981. *Michael J. Collins*

Left: Class 58 was BR's own design of heavy-freight locomotive. No 58 016 heads a northbound rake of empty HAAs past Hasland, Chesterfield, on 12 July 1990. *John Chalcraft / Rail Photoprints*

Below:
No adhesion problems for Class 59 No 59 002 *Yeoman Enterprise* as it takes the 11.15 Purfleet–Merehead empties through Calthorp, on the Newbury line, on 6 March 1987. *D. E. Canning*

Right: The last British-designed and -built diesel-locomotive type was the Class 60. Numbering 100, the class operated widely across the network. On 23 July 2008 No 60 007 was in charge of the 18.38 Immingham–Santon ore train, photographed at Barnetby East Junction.
John Chalcraft / Rail Photoprints

Below: Freightliner Class 66/6 No 60 602 at Edale in the Hope Valley. Locomotives of the '66/6' sub-class have lower traction-motor gearing to improve performance on heavy freights.
Freightliner

Above left and right: The new Voith Maxima 4,000hp diesel-hydraulic prototype, representing the company's first foray into locomotive production. *Voith*

Below: Freightliner Class 70 No 70 001. At the time of writing (November 2010) initial teething troubles, primarily with the power unit, are being resolved, and reports suggest that this will be a very strong locomotive. *Freightliner*

12

CONCLUSIONS

The findings of this book are based on high-level official records, which are available to the public in the National Archives. These records have been supported by reference to technical papers delivered to the Institution of Locomotive Engineers and on consultation with key engineers at Voith and on the Western Region.

What has been deduced? The idea of trying diesel-hydraulic transmission in the main-line locomotive fleet started with the BTC's Central Staff in 1953, not with the Western Region in 1955. Any obstruction by the Central Staff to the Western Region's desire for a 'V200' scaled down for the British loading-gauge arose primarily because it would have been unacceptable politically in 1955, 10 years after the end of World War 2, for a nationalised undertaking to be importing German machinery if the equivalent could be built in Britain. This difficulty was overcome by setting up licensing agreements between German manufacturers and British engineering companies. In short, the BTC wished to try hydraulic drive; it was sensible to confine the trial to a single region, and the Western Region was the best choice and wanted to assess this form of propulsion.

It has also been illuminating to find absolutely no reference in the available papers to the Western Region's discounting diesel-electric traction because it could not cope with the haulage of trains over the South Devon banks. The maximum loads assigned to the different classes shows no advantage to diesel-hydraulic, because it was the factor of adhesion that proved to be the determining factor in this context.

At the time when the diesel-hydraulic classes were designed, there was a lack of appreciation, most notably at Swindon, about the full implications of torsional stresses. This led to major problems, notably with the 'D1000' class, that were never fully overcome and brought about shorter component life

than was achieved in Germany. This, of course, pushed up the cost of maintenance, which was exacerbated by the high cost of importing parts from Germany (and the associated long lead time); it also led to a high cost of any overhaul and repair work carried out at Swindon Works, in comparison with other British Railways shops. If any single issue has emerged as the key factor in the downfall of the diesel-hydraulic classes of the 1950s and 1960s, it is that Swindon was the core cause. By common consent, in discussion at the proceedings of the Institution of Locomotive Engineers, the Design Office did not sufficiently understand the implications of torsional stresses and the need to check them at the prototype stage, while the cost base of the works priced itself (and the locomotives it maintained) out of contention when spare capacity in British Railways' fleet enabled withdrawals to be made.

The financial equation of keeping a fleet of diesel-hydraulic locomotives in traffic quite simply grew to be the key issue. British Railways was running a commercial railway, not an over-sized train set, and budgetary factors forced it to look towards what offered best value, which turned out (in the second half of the 1960s) to be diesel-electric transmission for mixed-traffic main-line locomotives. Regrettably, this point is often conveniently overlooked outside professional railway circles. Let us not forget that it was the search for economy that drove the pre-nationalisation railway companies to look to diesel to replace steam. A desire to standardise on as few classes as possible, again for economy in operation and maintenance, meant that there was no reason to build any more main-line diesel-hydraulics after the 'D1000' order had been fulfilled.

Did hydraulic drive work in Britain? Well, in 1961 even J. F. Harrison conceded that neither form of transmission had any particular advantage over the other, though the report produced by his department on the subject in 1965 was clearly biased in its conclusions towards diesel-electric — in particular the BR/Brush Type 4.

There is no doubt that the early years of the 1960s coloured engineers' views about the diesel-hydraulics, because of the technical issues that emerged after the various classes had been in traffic for only a short time. In terms of the transmission (rather than the engines) these issues were largely resolved, and this enabled the 'D7000s' to be the third-most-reliable main-line diesel during the period after 1964, surpassed only by English Electric's 'D6700' and 'D8000' classes. The 'D1000s' too put in a higher annual mileage than any other Type 4 right up to the mid-1970s, though there was by then little to choose in this respect between them and the high-mileage English Electric Class 50s. Their availability too was latterly at least a match for the 'D1500s', which spent much less time on express passenger work and so should have returned better availability, at least on the bases argued in the CME's 1965 report, which compared the transmission types.

No more appropriate way to conclude this book can be found than to quote this prophetic passage from *Diesel Railway Traction* for 23 February 1934:

> The high-power diesel locomotive of the future will be fitted with a combination of direct drive and electric or pneumatic transmission, … but in view of the Voith/Sinclair drive it appears that, as far as railcars are concerned, hydraulic media have a distinct future.

Remaining in production until 1967, BR's own design of Type 2 diesel-electric went through several changes but was never the best performer in its power range, and the last examples were retired 20 years later.
On 15 August 1983 an unidentified Class 25 coasts out of Disley Tunnel with loaded limestone hoppers from the ICI quarry at Tunstead bound for the Northwich works sidings at Oakleigh. *Gavin Morrison*

BIBLIOGRAPHY

Clough, David N.: *BR Standard Diesels of the 1960s* (Ian Allan, 2009)
Diesel Pioneers (Ian Allan, 2005)
Dow, George: *Great Central Railway, Vol 3* (Ian Allan, 1959)
Haresnape, Brian: *British Rail Fleet Survey 7: Diesel Shunters* (Ian Allan, 1984)
British Rail Fleet Survey 8: Diesel Multiple-Units — The First Generation (Ian Allan, 1985)
Harris, Roger: *The Allocation History of BR Diesels and Electrics, Vol 5* (published by the author, 2005)
Nock, O. S.: *History of the GWR, Vol 3* (Ian Allan, 1964)

The author has also consulted the following in the preparation of this book:

BTC and BR official papers in the National Archives
Issues of *Modern Railways*, the *Railway Gazette*, *The Railway Magazine* and *Trains Illustrated*
Proceedings of the Institution of Locomotive Engineers

Below: By any measure of success BR's own Type 4 design — the heaviest to run on Britain's railways — was not a front-runner, but over time these locomotives put in much useful work over an extensive part of the network. On 13 March 1977 Class 45/0 No 45 042 hurries through the tunnels at Kentish Town with the 13.45 St Pancras–Derby. *Les Nixon*